Lucy's Diary

The Journal of Lucy Rodd aged 15
during her visit to England in 1870

ISBN 978-09549137-8-6
ISBN 09549137-8-7

Published by
Polperro Heritage Press,
Clifton-upon-Teme, Worcestershire WR6 6EN
United Kingdom
www.polperropress.co.uk

Printed by
Biddles Ltd.
King's Lynn, Norfolk PE30 4LS
United Kingdom

Introduction

Lucy Rodd was just short of her fifteenth birthday when she began an epic journey from her hometown of Rockford, Illinois, to England and back in May 1870. Her travels took her by horse drawn wagon, train, ocean steamer and pony cart. Lucy recorded every day of her four month adventure in a handwritten journal.

Lucy traveled with her parents, Joseph and Mary Ann Rodd. They visited friends and relatives in England whom her parents had known before they immigrated to Rockford by way of Canada in 1853. Lucy was born in Rockford in 1855, the youngest of four surviving daughters (two others had died before 1870). Her parents had not been 'home' to England in 38 years.

For a young lady, Lucy had a perceptive way of observing the people she met and the various localities she visited with her parents. Her diary vividly describes many of the places and events in a way that makes the reader feel that they are with her on her trip. Her original style and sentence structure has been largely left unaltered although some explanatory notes have been added for modern readers on either side of the Atlantic.

MJS

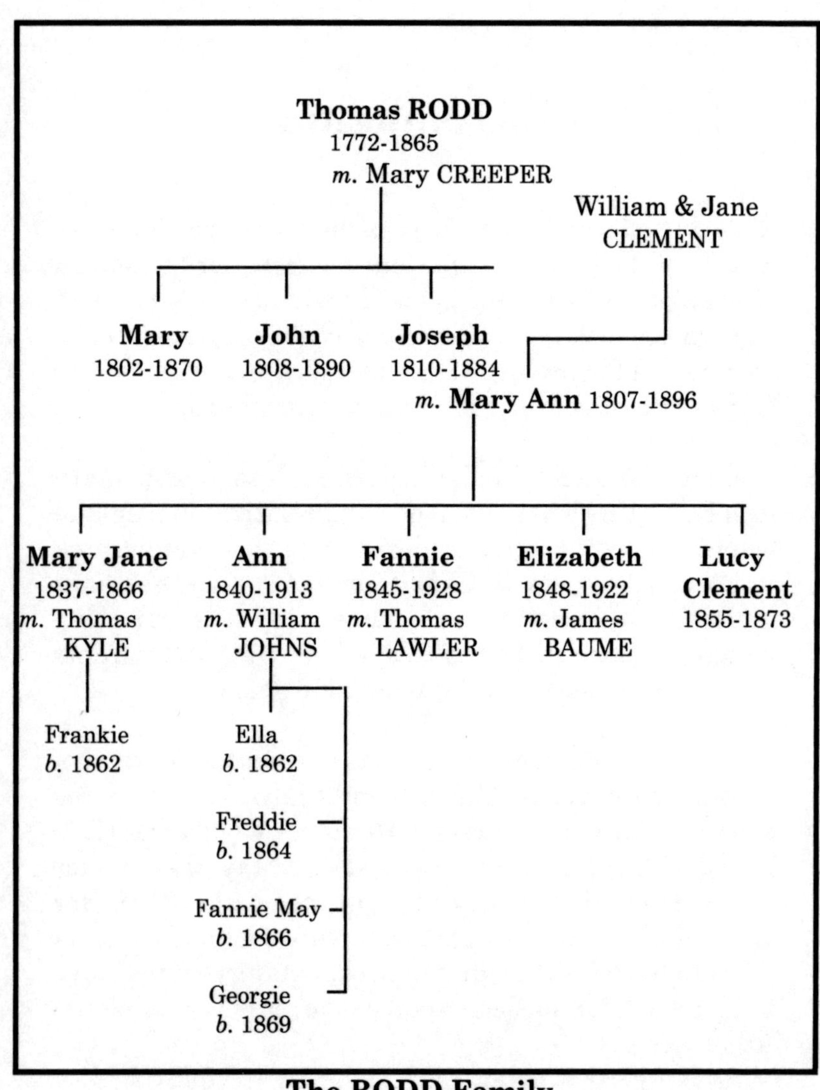

The RODD Family

The Journey Begins

Rockford, Monday May 2nd, 1870

As I, Lucy Rodd, am about to visit England I propose keeping a journal and when I return, I expect to take a great deal of satisfaction in reading it over.

This morning we were up by five o'clock, preparing all things necessary for our journey. Several friends called to see Pa and Ma. Mary Peck, Sarah and Jennie Lake called on me. We all felt sad at parting, but I shall only be gone about four months. The 'taxi' came for us at half past nine and bore us away from the 'brick house' over to the depot.

William,[1] Annie,[2] Thomas,[3] and Fannie[4] rode over in the carriage to bid us 'good bye'. The train soon started, bound for the city of Chicago and bearing us far away from the dear ones at home.

I did not enjoy the ride, for while every time I thought of <u>home</u>, there was a queer sensation in my throat and it was impossible to keep the tears from my eyes. At noon we stopped at Elgin, but we brought <u>our</u> dinner

1. William Johns, married to Lucy's sister Ann [neé Rodd}, living in Rockford, Illinois, USA.
2. Sister Ann [neé Rodd] Johns, married to William Johns.
3. Thomas Lawler, married to Lucy's sister Fannie [neé Rodd], Rockford, Illinois.
4. Sister Fannie [neé Rodd] Lawler, married to Thomas Lawler.

from home and I enjoyed it more for that. Dr. Kerr and lady were in the same car, traveling east. At one of the stations he got off, and then went into the smoking car, but his wife did not know it and so thought he had been left behind and had just decided to telegraph back to see, when he came back, so we had a laugh over it.

About three o'clock we arrived in Chicago, where we met Mr. [James] Baume[5]. About four, we left for Evanston and arrived there about five o'clock. Ma and myself rode to the 'Parsonage' in a cab, and Pa and Mr. Baume walked up. Sister Lizzie[6] met us at the door and we were very glad to see each other. They were all well and like living in Evanston very much. The Parsonage is a good large house, prettily situated and nicely furnished. After tea, Lizzie, Pa, Ma and myself went down to the lake [Michigan]. The wind was blowing quite hard and made the lake pretty rough. I thought it was fearfully grand. There were several little rowboats out on the water and I can assure you, I did not envy their occupants any. In the evening I played on the organ for a lady that called to see Ma and sister Lizzie.

Evanston, Tuesday May 3rd, 1870

This morning I feel first rate, not near as tired as I did last night. Pa and Ma say they feel a little homesick but I do not. I am just beginning to enjoy myself, for that funny sensation in my throat is quite gone now when I think of home. Mr. Baume hired a livery carriage and horses and took Lizzie, Pa, Ma and myself out riding. We went to see Heck Hall and the University. They are both magnificent buildings standing in the same grounds overlooking the lake. I think the situation is splendid.

5. Rev. James Baume, Lucy's brother-in-law, married to her sister, Elizabeth [Lizzie] of Evanston, Illinois.
6. Sister, Elizabeth [neé Rodd] Baume, married to Rev. James Baume.

We all had a drink of water from a well in the grounds. It was nice pure water and real cold.

The lake was very calm and still, not a bit like it was last night. Mr. Baume told us why Heck Hall was so called. It was named after an Irish woman called Barbara Heck who reclaimed some backslidden men into the first Methodists. At Heck Hall the students of the University prepare for the ministry. The old University is used as a Preparatory and the old Heck Hall as boarding house for the students. Then we drove down to the Rosehill Cemetery. It is a lovely place and does not seem like a place of the dead. Some of the monuments are beautiful, especially the 'Fireman's'. The stone of Bishop Hamlin, is very fine, but is quite plain, for there is nothing but his name on it. We also visited Calvary, or the Catholic cemetery, there are some very fine monuments there too. On the children's graves they have a notion of putting on their toys and play things, some of the graves are completely covered with them. I think it looks rather queer, but I suppose it is because the parents hold them very sacred.

On our way back we called on Mrs. Nate but did not stay long for she was very sick. Her mother Mrs. Leonard of Chicago was there with her. We arrived home just in time for dinner and we had asparagus and cranberry pie. After dinner I amused myself in Mr. Baume's study for several hours, looking at pictures and curiosities and reading. Just before tea, Lizzie, Mr. Baume, Pa, Ma and myself went over to the University and went through the principal rooms. We went in the chapel, classrooms, president's library, students library and museum. The latter has a very nice collection of curiosities etc. Then we went up one hundred and sixty-two steps to the top of the tower. The scenery was splendid and we had such a nice view of the lake. I thought Evanston showed off to very good advantage. Some call it 'Paradise on earth' and I agree with them.

Evanston, Wednesday May 4th, 1870

This morning at half past nine the cab came for us and took us to the depot. We felt nearly as sad at parting from our friends here, as we did when we left home. When we arrived in Chicago, Mr. Leonard met us at the depot with his carriage and took us to his house. We found them all quite well, and Mrs. Leonard seemed quite pleased to see us. Her son is just of age and is a doctor. He sings and plays on the piano splendidly and presented me with a piece of sheet music entitled *Give The Boy A Chance*. It is real cute and the music is very good. I offered to pay for it but he would not take the money. We had a very pleasant time there and had all the candy I could eat and my pocket full besides. About four Mrs. Leonard took us to the depot and Mr. Baume came into Chicago to bid us 'good bye' and see us off. Well soon we were off, and going almost at the rate of lightening speed, bound for the city of New York. Near Michigan City, Indiana we passed a great many, very large sand hills and I almost wished I was a little child again and lived near there so I could play in the sand. At eight o'clock we stopped at Niles, Michigan, for supper.

Riding by rail towards New York, Thursday May 5th, 1870

This morning just after daylight we arrived in Detroit, Michigan. We could just see the sun rising in the east. The locomotive pushed the cars onto the boat and then left us. The Detroit river was very calm and still and I was not afraid one bit. It took us quite a while to cross, but at last we were safely landed on the other side of the river in Windsor and Chatham a town or village in the dominion of Canada. The land between Windsor and Chatham was very poor, I do not see how the farmers can raise enough to maintain themselves and families. We stopped at Chatham for refreshments but not long enough to get much. Pa got off to get a cup of coffee and just as he had commenced to drink it, the bell rang and the train started so Pa had to leave his coffee behind and jump on the train quickly. Eastward from this station the land was much better, the meadows and trees were very green, just as they were in Rockford, when we left there. But in Evanston, everything was far behind, the trees were just beginning to bud. I suppose the reason of it was because of the cold winds coming in from the lake. I have seen plenty of log houses since I came on the Canada side, some of them you could hardly call houses but rather huts. I think the pine groves were beautiful, the trees were so green. I should like to live right in the center of one of those groves.

This side of London, Canada, is a great oil district and we saw a great many large oil vats. At half past eight, we arrived in London and stopped thirty minutes for breakfast, which I enjoyed very much for I was beginning to get hungry. There was such a crowd around the depot, we could hardly get to the eating rooms, for two companies of volunteers got on here, and the band played till the train started. The volunteers were going to Red River. About half past ten we passed through Lynden, the place where Cousin Delia lives but we did not see anyone we knew. Most of the fences round here were stump fences and they looked so queer. Around Dundas and Hamilton the scenery was beautiful and Dundas was such a pretty little place. It is situated on a mountain that was nearly covered with pretty pine trees and at the foot of the mountain, a clear little stream runs along. We passed over the suspension bridge[7] and we could see the Niagara Falls but they did not show off to very good advantage but what we saw of them was grand. Lockport, New York was a real pretty place and had a nice large school house and several other large buildings. A clear little stream runs through the place on which was situated several nice large buildings. About five o'clock we arrived in Rochester, New York. It is a large place and has a great many large and handsome buildings and a nice large depot where we stopped fifteen minutes to change engines. Rochester is situated on the Genesee river and is noted for its extensive flour mills. Its product is from 600,000 to 1,000,000 barrels of flour per annum. At half past eight we arrived in Syracuse, a place noted for its salt works, we saw a great many salt manufactories. We stopped here thirty minutes for supper.

New York, Friday May 6th, 1870

This morning about seven o'clock we arrived in the city of New York. We went to French's Hotel and ate a good breakfast, then went down to the wharf number forty five where the Inman Line[8] steamers land. We found that the *City of Antwerp*[9] sails tomorrow so we examined the cabins and secured a couple. After dinner we rode through the principal streets and saw some fine buildings five and six stories high built of iron and stone.

7. The Railway Suspension Bridge built for the Grand Trunk Railway to connect Canada to the United States, 1855-1877.
8. Inman Line was formed in 1850 and added steerage berths to their ships for emigrant trade in 1852.
9. The *City of Antwerp* was built for the Inman Line in 1867 for transatlantic voyages. Tonnage 2391, length 332 feet, breadth 39.4 feet clipper stem, one funnel, 3 masts, iron construction, single screw, and a top speed of 12 knots. She went missing in November 1890; it is presumed she struck an iceberg and sank with the loss of 43 lives on board.

Journey At Sea

New York, Saturday May 7th, 1870

This morning after eating a hearty breakfast we took our things and went down to the steamer so as to get settled before it started. On the wharf Pa bought four nice large beaded pin cushions. One is for his sister, one for Ma's sister and one for each of Cousin Thomas's sisters. The *City of Antwerp* is a very large steamer and burns from seventy five to eighty tons of coal in twenty-four hours. There are five cooks and two bakers. There are nearly one hundred crew, including the officers. The captain and mates are real polite and gentlemanly, especially the captain, and all the other officers and sailors take off their hats when in his presence.

The dining saloon and cabins were handsomely furnished and I expect I shall enjoy myself finely. About ten o'clock, the sailors weighed anchor, the bell rang and we began to move slowly from the shore of beloved America toward Old England and leaving behind us all our dear friends and relations and bearing me far away from the land of my birth, to new and other scenes from what I have been accustomed to, but not to Pa and Ma for we are going to the land of their childhood. We got out of sight of land in an hour and a half.

During the afternoon we passed several ships, one was a 'man of war', another was a French ship. At one o'clock we had lunch, but it was more like a dinner then a lunch. We have a very strong southeast wind and the sea is rather rough but I think it is grand, and after lunch I remained up on deck, looking at the water dashing up against the side of the steamer and watching the foam. About four o'clock, just as the dinner bell rang, I began to be initiated into the mysteries of sea sickness and I can not begin to describe my feelings at that moment but if you want to know what they were, why the best way for you to do is to cross the ocean and be sea sick yourself. The stewardess helped me get to my berth for I was not able to do it myself. The stewardess was a nice matronly looking person and filled her place well.

At Sea, Sunday May 8th, 1870

Today Pa, Ma and myself remained in our berths all day and we were just as weak and sick as could be. There were services in the dining saloon, but I guess there was not a very large congregation present for more then half of the cabins passengers are sick. The whole number of cabin passengers is fifty, and the number of steerage passengers about seventy five. The sea was very boisterous all day and the steamer rocked and rolled very much.

Torsnow, the captain, told us how far we had gone since yesterday noon and it was two hundred and sixty four miles. I almost believe if I had known I should be so sick I should have been inclined to have remained at home but then if I had not come I should not have been able to form any idea what ever of the grandeur of the ocean, so I am glad I came after all. I have not eaten anything all day neither has Ma. The captain says we are sailing at the rate of about twelve miles an hour or a mile in five minutes.

At Sea, Monday May 9th, 1870

This morning we all felt a little better and Ma and I gathered up courage enough to dress but I laid down in the ladies' saloon all day. Pa did not get up. I did not eat much today either. From yesterday noon until today noon we traveled three hundred and eighty miles. In the afternoon I felt worse again so I retired early.

At Sea, Tuesday, May 10th, 1870

This morning I felt a little better so Pa helped Ma and me up on deck for I was too weak to go up alone. I remained up on deck all day and the little I ate, I had taken up to me. Today noon the number of miles we sailed in the last twenty four hours was two hundred and two miles. We saw several sailing vessels today, but no steamers. The sailors hoist the flags every time they see a ship or steamer and are answered back in the same way.

At Sea, Wednesday May 11th, 1870

I remained all day up on deck today also. During the day we saw several ships most of them were bound for New York. In the afternoon we saw a whale, way off in the distance spouting up water, and it created quite a sensation among the passengers. Several times afterwards a gentleman would call out "a whale" and all would get up and look to where he pointed and say "where, where" but we soon found out that it was only a sell. From yesterday noon till today noon the number of miles we sailed was three hundred and two miles.

At Sea, Thursday May 12th, 1870

Today I feel much better and more like myself. I remained up on deck all day for every time I go below I am worse. For breakfast Johnny brought me up some toast and lemonade. Johnny is the ladies' cabin boy. This is his first voyage so he is not acquainted with ways of the steamer yet and he acts quite stupid about some things. His father is dead or is supposed to be for he was one of the crew of the *City of Boston*[1] at the time it was lost. The captain's cabin boy is a real smart black haired little fellow and has followed the sea for three years. Today we sailed two hundred and eighty three miles.

At Sea, Friday May 13th, 1870

It is very squally today and like April weather. The officers made a tent large enough for all that wished to remain up on deck. I amused myself most all day from a book out of the library. Most of the passengers have recovered to enjoy themselves finely. I did not go down to my meals today either but had them brought up to me. I remained up on deck until real late for the moon was shining so brightly and I enjoyed it so much. I did not go below until after ten o'clock. We sailed two hundred and eighty six miles.

At Sea, Saturday May 14th, 1870

Today I feel nearly well again and managed to eat breakfast and dinner with the rest. Today also we had April weather so I remained down in the ladies' cabin and had a nice time reading. I am just beginning to enjoy myself and Miss Sarah Webster and myself have famous times. She is about my own age and so is Miss Griffin but I do not like her as well for she was so very rude and boisterous. She is now on her way to Paris and is going to school to the convent for a few years. Today we sailed two hundred and eighty six miles. Tonight also, the moon shone out very bright and clear.

1. *City of Boston* was an Inman steamer lost at sea in March 1870 from unknown causes.

At Sea, Sunday May 15th, 1870

Today I managed to go down to breakfast, lunch, dinner and tea. There were services today also. Pa and Ma attended them but I remained down in the cabin. After dinner it rained a little but cleared off again before night and the moon shone out brightly.

At Sea, Monday May 16th, 1870

We had a very stormy cold wind today. It was so cold, we could not remain up on deck. As I feel pretty well today and have not anything to read, I will amuse myself by writing out a list of the good things we have to eat at each meal. First in the morning at six o'clock we have toast and tea or coffee. Breakfast at nine and it generally lasts three quarters of an hour. We have cold beef and ham, fried ham and eggs, beefsteak, potatoes boiled or fried, cold tongue, toast and butter, tea and coffee.

Lunch at twelve, it consisted of vegetable soup, fish, all kinds of cold meat, potatoes, bread and cheese. Dinner from four until six o'clock. This important meal consisted of several kinds of soup, fish, all kinds of meat cold or boiled, roasted, baked, stewed or fried. Pigs head and feet, calves head and feet, head cheese and sausage, also turkey, chicken and pigeon. Vegetables such as potatoes, tomatoes, turnips, carrots, asparagus, cabbage, and nettles and green peas. We had several kinds of soup such as pea soup, kidney soup, mock turtle soup, vegetable soup and beef too. We also had almost every kind of pickles. Then we had chicken pie, beefsteak pie and veal pie. Then came the pastry including every thing in that line you could think of with and without a name. Then bread and cheese and then came the fruit such as pineapples, oranges, raisins, figs and three kinds of nuts.

About half past seven we had bread or toast and butter, jelly or preserves and tea or coffee. Supper at nine o'clock and you could have either bread and cheese or bread and meat. Now is not all that enough for one day? I think so.

Yesterday we sailed three hundred and two miles. Today we sailed three hundred and eight miles. In the evening it rained real hard and the sea was very rough and made the steamer rock a great deal so I stayed in the ladies' saloon and sang a few pieces for the girls.

At Sea, Tuesday May 17th, 1870

About three o'clock this morning we came in sight of Old Ireland but it was so foggy we could not see much until about eight. Then we could see some sign of life on both land and sea. About half past eight we entered Queenstown[2] harbor. The tender came out to us and took a few passengers and their baggage to Queenstown. They also took on board the corpse of a man from the steerage that died last night at twelve o'clock of the dropsy.[3] He had lived in New York for several years but he wished to go home to see his mother so he left his wife, children and friends and started for Ireland with his sister but he died three hours before we came in sight of his home.

We remained in the beautiful harbor over three hours waiting for the tender to come and pull us out for there was so many vessels and boats in the way that our big steamer could not turn around. When we started, I felt

2. Queenstown was a seaport in County Cork, on the south shore of Ireland. When Queen Victoria visited in 1849 the town was renamed in her honour to Queenstown, but reverted to Cobb in 1922 after Ireland gained its independence.

3. Dropsy is commonly known today as Congestive Heart Failure where the patient has an abnormally large amounts of fluid on the lungs.

that awful feeling of sea sickness come over me again, but I am happy to say it did not last long. After lunch I went up on deck and watched the water for a long time. I love to watch the water; great waves dashing up against the steamer and then break into foam forming mountain-like ridges of purest white snow. After dinner we passed the steamer *Virginia* of the National Line. It left New York three days before the *City of Antwerp* did and the captain says we shall reach the bar before her. Today we sailed three hundred and two miles.

At Sea, Wednesday May 18th, 1870

This morning about three o'clock we saw the first sight of Old England. It looked so cold and dreary and when Ma first saw it she exclaimed, "America for ever" and I fully agreed with her. About four o'clock we reached the sand bar where we dropped anchor and waited nearly six hours for the turn of the tide. The captain said if we had been twenty minutes sooner we could have crossed over. This morning at the breakfast table we had no fear of having our plates tipped off into our laps and our cup of hot coffee sliding off toward the young lady or gentleman sitting on your right, for our steamer was at a stand still. After breakfast when I went up on deck we could just see the *Virginia* coming in sight. About ten o'clock our brave steamer started again. After we passed the bar we had yet fifteen miles to go which took us over an hour. Since leaving Queenstown we have traveled two hundred and forty-five miles. In all we have sailed three thousand two miles.

About eleven o'clock we could see the great city of Liverpool but its looks did not charm me any for it was so smoky. About a mile out from the city the sailors dropped anchor and the tender came and took us to land. Just before leaving the steamer, the captain and mates went around and shook hands with all of the cabin passengers, and when we left they gave us three hearty cheers. Well at last we got safely to land and a happy landing it was too, especially to those who were greeted by friends and relations, but there was no such good luck in store for us, for no one in England knew of our intending to visit that country. As soon as we landed, our trunks passed under the inspection of the Customs house officers and then sent off to the Sarme Street depot and we soon followed.

Pa had just time to get the tickets and secure our seats when the train started. As soon as we left the depot or station, we went through a very long dark tunnel and the lights were not lit either. As soon as we were in the light again an engine was fastened to the cars and we were soon off again bound for Instow in good earnest and going almost at lightning speed through tunnels, over bridges and cross-tracks, it made no difference which, and sometimes it seemed as if we would certainly go off the track.

The cars are such funny little things. They call them carriages or vans, and are divided into first, second and third classes. The carriages are divided by partitions into four or five compartments, with a door and two windows in each end and two long seats extending all the length of the compartment. The passengers sit face to face as in an omnibus and ten persons can ride in each compartment. The first class carriages have seats cushioned with velvet nearly up to the top of the compartment, and there are curtains for the windows. In the second class the seats are cushioned with black oil cloth but in the third class there are no cushions at all. There are no conveniences in either class and the trains do not stop at the depot for refreshments so it is rather bad for anyone traveling very far, but <u>we</u> happened to have food with us, so we were all right. I have seen these English cars described as prisons on wheels.

In this part of the country the scenery is lovely for the land is very mountainous so we have plenty of long dark tunnels to enter but we always find the light again. There are not many fences <u>here</u> as we have at home but stone walls take their place. In some places there are pretty little white thorn trees planted along on top of the walls and they looked real pretty. Every place we pass people seemed to have a great taste for flowers, for every house we pass is almost surrounded with them. I think the stacks and wall flowers are very pretty and they smell so fragrant. The latter flowers will grow anywhere, even on top of buildings and on the stone walls.

We passed through several important cities such as Birmingham, Worcester, Gloucester, Bristol, Taunton, Exeter and Barnstaple beside a number of places of smaller note. Near Birmingham there were a great many brick yards, and the houses seemed to be all made of red brick. We arrived in Bristol about eight o'clock in the evening. There we changed cars for Exeter where we arrived about half past ten and remained there until morning, for there was no train going to Instow that night.

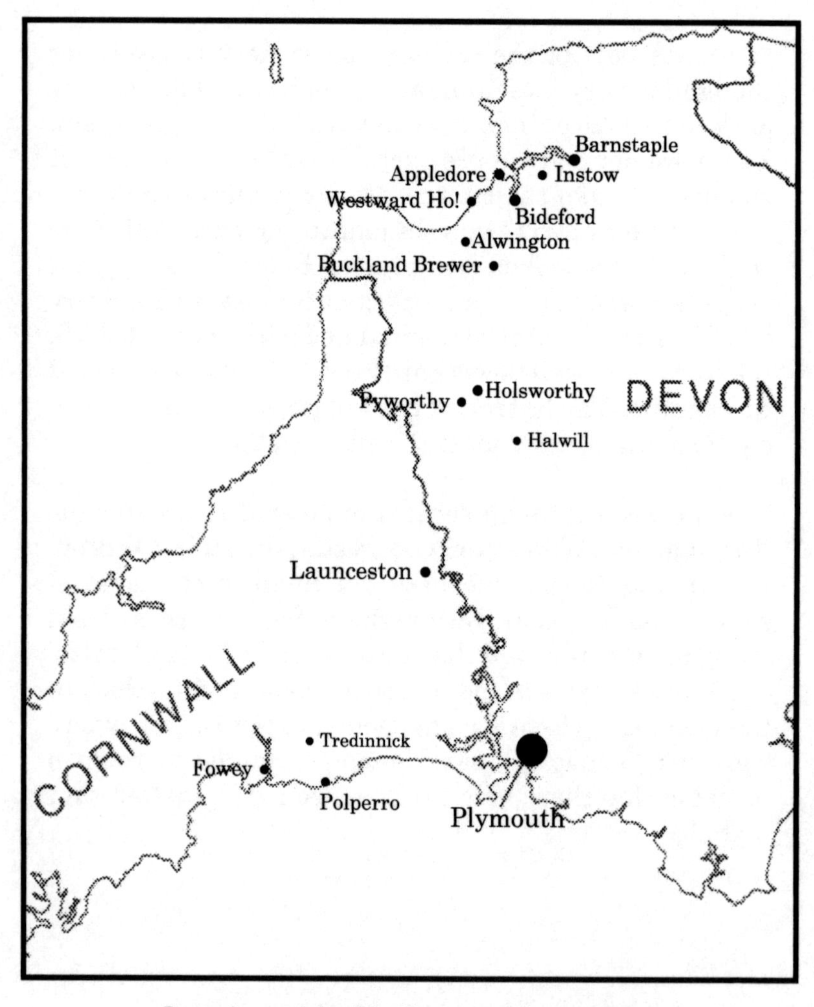

Locations visited by Lucy and her parents during their visit to Devon and Cornwall

Arrival in England

Instow, Devonshire, Thursday May 19th, 1870

This morning we left Exeter on the three o'clock train for Instow. We arrived there about half past six, and went to a hotel and changed our dusty garments then ate a hearty breakfast. Pa asked the landlord if he knew a Mr. [John] Rodd living near, but first he asked him other questions so he would not suspect who we were, but Pa was not cautious enough for the landlord replied, "Yes I know Mr. Rodd well and <u>you are his brother</u>." Then Pa went over to Uncle John's and asked for Thomas [Rodd] but he was not at home so Pa made known to them who he was. Uncle John and Aunt Sarah [Rodd] did not know Pa at first but he knew them. Cousin Mary Ann [Rodd] came back to the hotel with Pa to see us and we went home with her and received a very hearty welcome.

Thomas and Fannie [Rodd] are gone to Pyworthy where Aunt Mary [Gerry] lived. She died the day before we landed and it made Pa feel very sad for he had strong hopes of seeing his only sister once more. I think Uncle John looks so much like Pa and sometimes I think whether it is Pa or not. Aunt Sarah is Uncle's second wife and I like her first rate. She is a good motherly person and treats my cousins as if they were her own children. Mary Ann is the youngest. She is rather tall, fair, fat but not for forty, but nineteen. I think she looks a great deal like sister Annie. She has rather light hair and complexion, and blue eyes. In the afternoon Fannie came home. She is real short, has a dark complexion, and jet black hair and eyes. Thomas is neither very tall or very short and his hair is neither light or dark but altogether brown.

After dinner Ma wrote a letter home and Mary Ann and I took it to the Post Office. Instow is situated on the river Torridge near its mouth. The tide goes up the river for about ten miles, twice a day and when it goes back it leaves two or three miles of nice clean sand near Instow with beautiful little shells scattered over it. After going to the Post Office Cousin and I went down to the beach, and picked up some of the pretty shells. The tide was just coming in and it was real amusing as well as interesting to watch it creeping in so slowly for awhile then it would give a sudden start and come in a long way real fast. I compared it to a cat creeping on slowly and slyly after a mouse.

After we went back, Pa, Ma, Uncle and myself went up on the hills and through the meadows and orchard and I enjoyed it very much. I gathered a bouquet of pretty wild flowers and kept them three or four days. In the evening we went out for a walk and then I had a nice time with the pet lamb two weeks old.

Instow, Friday May 20th, 1870

This morning we remained in the house and rested ourselves for we were very tired. After dinner Ma, Fannie and I went out riding with the pony and cart or trap. The traps are such queer little two-wheeled concerns and they are the most abominable vehicle ever invented. While riding in one of them it is impossible to keep your seat and you are in great danger of being shaken to pieces, even on the smooth roads of Old England. We went up the high road and saw the chapel and some nice residences then came back round by the sea and down the low road to Uncles. After we came back, Pa, Ma, Mary Ann and I went down on the beach. I took my basket and picked up some more pretty shells. For tea they always butter the bread before putting it on the table and they only have bread, butter and cake for tea in this part of England. After tea Thomas came home. Mary Ann, Fannie and I went over to the depot to meet him. It is only a few steps from Uncle's so we did not have far to go. I put on my veil and did not speak first but he knew me and said, "That veil cannot hide you, Miss Lou." When we got home he searched all over for Pa and Ma and at last found them. Thomas was not as much surprised to see us as we thought he would be for a gentleman he was acquainted with in Bideford heard we had come and he told Thomas of it. On the half past eight train Fannie and I went into Bideford to get her mourning garments to attend Aunt Mary's funeral.

Bideford looked to be quite a large place but I could not tell very much about the size of it as it was night. It is situated on both sides of the river Torridge, about three miles south of Instow. Fannie was ready to go back by ten o'clock so we walked back to the station where Thomas was waiting with the pony and trap to take us back to Uncle John's or home as I am beginning to call it. It took us nearly an hour to drive the three miles so it was about eleven o'clock when we got home.

Instow, Saturday May 21st, 1870

This morning Pa, Ma and myself went down on the sands and watched the tide coming in a long while. On the half past one train Pa, Ma, Thomas and myself went into Bideford. This place is about half the size of Rockford, though it looks larger for the greater part of the place is built on the side of a high hill, so it shows itself off nicely. All through England on one or two days of each week, the farmers meet in a large building built for the purpose and sell their vegetables and meat to all who wish to buy them. They call this day Market Day. We went through the market house and saw there, cousins Robert and Charles Withecombe and their wives.

The inhabitants of Bideford seem to think me a great curiosity or at least my clothes are, for everybody looks at me so. While passing down one street, a colored gentleman, standing in a doorway stared at me as if I was something very wonderful indeed, and I heard him call his wife to come to the door and see my shoes. They wear very low ones here and I suppose my high ones look as queer to them as their low ones do to me, but I do not stare quite as rudely as they do I hope. One little girl had the impoliteness to stoop down and look at my shoes. I suppose she wanted to find out how high they extended. But I enjoyed being odd here where I am but little known, it is fun to see nearly everyone looking at me.

We went back to Instow on the half past four train. After tea Pa, Ma, Mary Ann and myself went down to the sands again and walked up and down the beach for a long time. There was scarcely any wind so the water was quite still and we all enjoyed ourselves very much for it was such a beautiful moonlight evening. There are very few lamps used in this part of England but tallow[2] candles are used in their place. When we got home from the beach Mary Ann and I had a nice little walk up past the chapel then back around by the sea and down the low road to Uncle John's again. Today Uncle and Fannie went to Aunt Mary's funeral.

2. Tallow candles are made from the rendered fat of cattle or sheep.

Instow, Sunday May 22nd, 1870

This morning Pa, Ma, Aunt, Thomas and myself went up to the chapel and heard a very good sermon preached by Ma's cousin, Christopher Clement. The churches are all hundreds of years old and belong to the Episcopalians, the Dissenters' places of worship are called chapels. On Sundays in small towns and country places, the services are conducted by local preachers. The churches have stationed ministers. Some of the churches are very old, some of them were built when the laborers worked for one penny of English money a day. Preaching here in the morning commences at eleven o'clock and closes at twelve. In the evening it commences at six and closes at half past seven.

When we returned home, Ma's sister Fannie and husband [William Withecombe] and Cousin Ellen and Robert [Withecombe] was there. Aunt Fannie looks a good deal like Ma, and looks at least two years older then her although she is that much younger. Uncle William Withecombe is quite fleshy and, if I may be allowed to write that unladylike expression, is real jolly looking. Ellen is slim and rather tall, has jet black hair and eyes. I think she looks a little like Sister Lizzie. Aunt Fannie remained talking with Ma all the afternoon and Uncle and cousins went to see some friends living in Fremington, a little place about three miles from Instow.

After dinner Mary Ann and I went walking up past the chapel then up through a long narrow lane by the church. Then we went across two or three fields and down over a very steep hill. From the top of this hill the scenery was lovely. We could see all of Instow, also Appledore, a little fishing port just across the river from Instow. In the evening Pa, Mary Ann and myself went to chapel. After service Mary Ann and a few of her young friends and myself went walking. We went way up the Bideford road a long way then back to the chapel and back around to Uncles. We had a very pleasant walk and I enjoyed it very much. After we got back I sang a few pieces for Aunt Sarah from the *Fresh Laurels* then I sang *Farewell Good Night.*

Instow, Monday May 23rd, 1870

This morning we were so tired we did not go anywhere until half past twelve. Then Pa, Ma, Mary Ann and myself went to Bideford and Ma bought herself a black silk dress. Pa, Ma and I went back to Uncle's by the half past four train, but Mary Ann was not ready to go then so she walked home. She got home while we were eating supper. She said she was only three minutes too late for the cars. In the evening it was quite cool and very pleasant. At half past seven Pa, Ma and Mary Ann went to chapel. I did not go for I had a severe headache. They were gone nearly an hour.

Instow, Tuesday May 24th, 1870

This morning Pa, Ma, Thomas and myself went up in the fields on the hill and I gathered a few pretty wild flowers. When we returned I amused myself by watching the trains pass, from the sitting room window up stairs. About fifteen trains pass here each day. At half past one, Pa, Ma, Thomas and myself went into Bideford again. I am sure I ought to know the way there pretty soon and know all about the place too for I go there so often.

Pa, Ma and myself went back to Uncle's on the half past four train and Thomas rode home with a friend. After tea Ma and I went to the Post Office and posted a letter to Mr. Odgers, then I went with Mary Ann to feed the pet lamb. It ran to meet us as soon as we called "Tibby Tibby". When we started for home Tibby wanted to go too, so we had to hurry and get outside the gate.

Instow, Wednesday May 25th, 1870

This morning Pa, Ma and I went down on the beach and watched the tide coming in. We saw three men fishing with their nets, but I am sorry to say they did not catch anything. After dinner I wrote a long letter to Jennie Lake, then took it to the Post Office.

This afternoon there was a great many cavalry passing here. They came from Barnstaple where they were trained last week. They looked very pretty sitting so straight on their horses and I watched them a long time from the window of the front room up stairs. One time while seven or eight were passing, I was looking out the window and one of them looked towards the house and said, "There are Americans in there," then he happened to see me and said, "There is one of them looking out of the window now." Then they all looked around at me, but I did not care one bit but rather proud to have them know that I am an American, but I do not see how they found it out.

After tea Mary Ann and myself had a nice long walk and talk in the garden. Then we went up in the meadow on the hill and fed the lamb and it wanted to come home with us again tonight. In the evening I printed a short note to Frankie [Kyle][3] and Ma wrote a long letter to sister Fannie.

Instow, Thursday May 26th, 1870

This morning directly after breakfast Pa, Ma, Thomas and myself got ready to go out for the day. The tide was out so we walked down to the river, then a boatman

3. Lucy's nephew (son of sister Mary-Jane Rodd and Thomas Kyle), raised in the Rodd household since being orphaned.

rowed us over to Appledore. There was scarcely any wind so the river was very still and I enjoyed our boat ride very much. Then we walked up through Appledore. It is built on the side of a steep hill overlooking the river Torridge. There is a very large dock yard and a great many sailing vessels anchor here.

I think the greater part of the inhabitants are fishermen and sailors with their families. From Appledore we had a very pleasant walk along the green lanes to Northam where cousin Martha [Main] lives. Well at last we got there and Mrs. Main [Martha's mother-in-law] met us at the gate with a very hearty welcome. We remained there an hour then Martha and her little girl [Eva Main] went riding with us. She has a Shetland pony and I think I never saw such a little one before and I just fell in love with it right off.

We rode about two miles behind the little pony to Westward Ho!.[4] It is a very pretty little watering place and a great many aristocrats go there. The hotels and boarding houses are splendid buildings and it costs more to live <u>there</u> than in <u>London</u>. Between Westward Ho! and the sea, there extends a pebble ridge about fifty feet wide at the bottom and gradually decreasing toward the top where it was about fifteen feet wide. The ridge is about thirty feet high and extends along by the sea for about four miles. It prevents the water from overflowing the land. At the bottom the ridge is composed of very large pebbles but gradually growing smaller towards the top, then they are very small. I suppose the ridge has been there for centuries for no one alive knows how it came there but it is supposed that it was washed up

4. Westward Ho! was named after the book of the same name by Charles Kingsley in 1855. The Holy Trinity church was built in the year of Lucy's visit.

by the sea at some very remote period and I think the Pebble Ridge[5] must be the eighth wonder of the world. I climbed over the ridge half a dozen times and outside of it we picked up some very pretty shells and pebbles from the rocks but the tide was coming in so we could not stay outside the ridge as long as we wanted to.

After leaving the sea we went up on a very high hill behind Westward Ho!. The scenery was just lovely and it was so nice and cool up there and we had a very refreshing drink of ginger beer. Then Pa and Thomas started back to Martha's for Pa was getting lame and we went to see the sand hills near one end of the ridge. It was real fun to run up and down them but some of them were pretty steep and the sand was rather loose. I picked up some very pretty little shells and shall take them home to Rockford. After walking all around the hills we started back to Martha's again. Pa and Thomas were back an hour before we were. Our long tramp on the sands sharpened up our appetites considerably so we ate hearty dinners. Soon after dinner Martha took us to Appledore with the pony and trap, then we walked down to the beach and the boatman rowed us over the river. The tide was in so he rowed us right up to the pier. After tea Mary Ann, Thomas and I took a nice walk.

Instow, Friday May 27th, 1870

This morning we were very tired but still, after breakfast, Pa, Ma, and myself went down to the beach and watched the tide going out and talked about home.

5. The 1879 Handbook for Travellers in Devonshire describes the Pebble Ridge as 'a long and wide barrier of large pebbles extending between the sea and the flat of Northam Burrows. This sandy, grassy plain is scarcely above the level of spring tide high water and would be exposed to destructive inundations if not for the natural pebble breakwater. The pebbles varying from ½ in. to a yard in diameter.' Today the Pebble Ridge is still a remarkable natural phenomenon and the pebbles are protected.

After dinner we went down again and stayed until half past four o'clock. This time we watched the tide coming in and I enjoyed it ever so much. After an early tea Pa, Ma, Thomas, Mary Ann and myself went for a walk up to Mrs. Cleveland's. She is a very rich lady and owns nearly all of the land around Instow and Bideford. We visited her private Park and it was just lovely there. The walks and flowers, summer houses and fish pond was so nice. We went in the summer house and sat down. It was just delightful and I hardly wanted to leave it again. Then we went up over a nice shady hill and saw the house. It was a very large one and showed itself off nicely.

Mrs. Cleveland's son fought in the Crimean War[6] in 1853 and was killed. On a very high hill near the house there is a very fine monument erected by his tenants in memory of him. We also saw the horse he had with him in the war. The scenery from this hill was splendid. We could see so far all around us. On our way back I picked some fern leaves and a few pretty wild bluebells. We all enjoyed our walk very much for the evening was so pleasant and cool. I think we chose just the right night for such a lovely walk.

Instow, Saturday May 28th, 1870

This morning I was rather tired but not enough so to remain in the house all day for after breakfast Pa, Ma and myself went down on the sands. The tide was out so we walked clear over to the river over the sands. On the half past one o'clock train Pa, Ma and myself went into Bideford. We went through the market and saw my cousins Robert and Charles Withecombe and Mrs. Main. They were quite well. We returned back to Instow on

6. The Crimean War (1853-1856) was fought between Russia and a group of nations including England, France, Turkey and Sardinia, on a peninsula on the north coast of the Black Sea in what is today the Ukraine.

the half past four o'clock train. After tea Mary Ann and myself went to the Post Office and got a letter for Ma from Mr. [John] Baume, Halifax, Yorkshire. They were all quite well and invited us to visit him before we returned home.

Instow, Sunday May 29th, 1870

This morning Pa and Mary Ann went to chapel. Ma and I was so tired and our feet were swollen so badly that we could not go and in fact we could not put on our shoes. After dinner I took a book and went down on the beach and read until after four o'clock. In the evening Pa, Mary Ann and myself went to the Eastleigh Sunday School Anniversary. Eastleigh is a little village about three miles from Instow. We heard a very good sermon preached and the singing also was very good and I enjoyed all of the exercises very much. I have the words of all the pieces they sung. The minister said that the winters are very rainy and disagreeable in England. Well I am glad that I do not live here then, for the winters in America are generally so clear and bright. The exercises were rather long and the chapel was well filled so it was pretty warm there, but our walk back to Uncle's was just splendid for it was a lovely evening and we all enjoyed it very much indeed or at least I enjoyed it.

Instow, Monday May 30th, 1870

This morning I went down on the beach again, although I have been down there so many times I am not tired of the grand old ocean yet and I presume I shall enjoy a good many more hours by its side. On the half past one train Mary Ann and myself went into Bideford. While we were gone it rained a little but stopped before we got home. We went back on the half past four train. Then Pa, Ma and myself went down on the beach and watched the tide coming in. It came in real fast and it looked real pretty. After tea I took a nice little walk alone.

Instow, Tuesday May 31st, 1870

This morning before breakfast Ma and myself was down on the beach a half an hour so we had a good appetite after breathing the sea air. While we were eating breakfast, Uncle came home with our first letter from Rockford. Sister Fannie and husband both wrote to us. They were all well but found it rather lonesome without us and Frankie keeps inquiring, "Will they come home soon" and we have been gone only one month, but that long has seemed a very long time to us while we did not get any letter from home, but I guess we shall be all right after this.

On the half past ten train Uncle and Pa went into Bideford. I amused myself until dinner time in the garden. My favorite place was a nice seat in the one corner of the garden shaded by honeysuckles. After dinner I commenced writing a letter to the inmates of a certain red brick house[7] in Rockford, and Ma wrote to sister Annie. Pa and Uncle came back on the half past three o'clock train. Uncle brought home some nice fresh strawberries from the market. They were the first of the season and were real nice large ones and they were just delicious with cream. Uncle gave eight pence a quart or about eighteen cents in American money. In the evening it was quite dreary and cold so we did not go anywhere but remained quietly in the house and talked about our dear friends in Rockford.

7. The 'red brick house' was Lucy's way of describing her home in Rockford (see page 5)

Lucy Clement Rodd (1855-1873)

Lucy with her parents, Mary Ann and Joseph Rodd

The Rodd family home in Rockford, Illinois

Lucy's sister Elizabeth (Mrs James Baume)

The *City of Montreal*, sister ship to the *City of Antwerp* that Lucy sailed on from New York in 1870

Lucy's mother, Mary Ann Rodd (left), sister Ann Johns (centre) and niece, Fannie May Brown with baby Orville, c1890

Instow, Wednesday June 1st, 1870

This morning Uncle brought us another letter from home. They were all well but had not received a letter from us yet, although we have written. We did not expect a letter today but still we were exceedingly glad to receive one. It was only thirteen days coming from home, but the one we received yesterday was nineteen days. After breakfast Ma and I finished our letters and Pa took them to the Post Office. All day it was very rainy and disagreeable outdoors and the wind blew real cold. After dinner Thomas and Mary Ann went to the Eastleigh Sunday School Tea Meeting. I had intended going if it had not rained. After tea Pa, Ma and myself went down on the beach a little while but we did not stay very long for it was still raining a little. Thomas and Mary Ann got home about ten o'clock. They said that they had a very pleasant time and there was a good many even if it did rain. I suppose they have so much rain in England that they get used to it.

Instow, Thursday June 2nd, 1870

This morning we remained in the house and rested. After dinner Pa, Ma and myself went down on the sands and walked a long, long way. I picked up a few very pretty shells. Pa says if I take <u>home</u> all the shells I pick up he will be obliged to charter a vessel to take them, but I guess it will not be quite as bad as <u>that</u>. After tea Mr. Withecombe, a friend of Ma's, took Pa Ma and myself boat riding with his wife and children. It was a lovely evening and we had a most delightful ride of about five miles. The little boy had his concertina[8] with him and he gave us some music. He played real good and I thought the music added ten fold to the pleasure of our ride.

8. A musical instrument similar to the accordion.

Instow, Friday June 3rd, 1870

This morning Pa, Ma, Thomas and myself took the nine o'clock train to Barnstaple.[9] It is situated about six miles north of Instow and is about the size of Rockford, and there are some very fine buildings there. The merchants and their families live over their establishments. In one of these large dry good stores Ma bought four colored silk dresses and a black silk sack etc. One of the dresses was for Sister Annie, one of them for Fannie, one for Lizzie and one for Ma and the other one and the sack for me. I think the dresses are handsome and I am very well suited with mine. We bought a real cute little farmer's satin suit for little Georgie [Johns]. The suit is drab and braided with white braid. Our day's purchases amounted to over twenty two pounds in English money or over one hundred and thirty dollars in American money. We returned to Instow by the four o'clock train having been gone several hours.

Instow, Saturday June 4th, 1870

This morning we did not go out anywhere. After dinner I strolled on the beach alone and picked up a few shells. For dinner we had a gooseberry fool and it was real good. Aunt told me how to make it - boil the gooseberries and add plenty of cream and sugar. In the evening we did not go anywhere but remained at home.

Instow, Sunday June 5th, 1870

I feel very well today though my throat is a little sore. This morning Pa, Ma, Mary Ann, Thomas, Uncle and I went to chapel and it was so warm today that I wore

9. Barnstaple is located on the Taw River estuary which is spanned by a 15 arch stone bridge dating form the 13th century. Barnstaple was the chief marketing town of north Devon and specialized in gloves, pottery, bricks, tiles, furniture, and lace and carried on a large woollen export trade with the American colonies.

my drab suit for a wonder. They have local preachers here and the one that spoke this morning was a young unmarried man. He preached a very good sermon from the text found in Romans (14th chapter, 10th verse). He described, or rather tried to describe the 'Judgment Day' and he described the signs that would precede that day. He spoke well and acted it out and entered into it with great earnestness. Now, have I not spoken well of him? But he deserves it all.

We had fig pudding[10] for dinner and it reminded me of last Christmas and New Year. In the afternoon Pa, Ma, Mary Ann and I took a walk up to the church for they have a church here too, but there was not any preaching so we had that walk for nothing, but we walked through the church and looked around a little and walked through the graveyard. We did not walk back as fast as we went for we were so warm. We were glad to get home. At six o'clock Ma, Aunt, Mary Ann and I went to chapel. Another gentleman preached tonight from Revelations (6th chapter, 8th verse) relating to death and hell. He preached a good sermon too and a rather long one. After we returned Mary Ann and I and a few of her young friends walked up to the lodge and back about two miles in all. One of the young ladies that went with us was a Miss Young, a very nice young person. Her father and mother are both dead and she lives with her grandparents, but they are not very good to her and I guess she has a pretty hard time. She is Russian and has three brothers in London. She is very pleasant and a real Christian. She is quite short, has light complexion and black hair and eyes. I think she is real pretty. I like her very much.

10. Probably plum pudding, a rich boiled or steamed pudding containing fruit and spices.

Instow, Monday June 6, 1870

This morning Pa, Ma, and myself went on the half past ten train to Bideford. If we had got there a few minutes sooner we would have gone to church for there were services held today and the 'Foresters' all marched to church. They all wore green sashes and they looked real pretty. The Foresters is a sort of club and once a year they meet and march through the principle streets and then go to church after which they parade the streets again. They looked very pretty dressed partly in green and the band played which reminded me very much of home.

We went back to Instow on the half past four train. For tea we had a junket[11] and it was real good. I do not know how it was made but there was plenty of rich cream used in the process. After tea Mary Ann and myself went out for a walk. Then we went down on the beach and around to the sand hills and saw the cricket house[12] and grounds and we had a real pleasant time.

Instow, Tuesday June 7th, 1870

I was real lazy this morning too, but my throat was quite sore and my head ached very much. When Uncle came from the Post Office this morning I asked him if he had got a letter, but 'no' he had not got any, but then I hardly expected any. How I would like to see all at home this beautiful morning, but they are not up yet for it is not four o'clock in the morning at home. I intended to have written to Jennie on Sunday, but I did not have the time; she would say ' that is not a very good excuse' but I cannot help it if she would.

11. Junket is a dessert of sweetened flavoured milk set with rennet.
12. The cricket house is the club house used for the game of cricket. Instow has one of England's oldest cricket clubs with a thatched club house roof.

At ten and one-half o'clock Pa, Ma and I went into Bideford and from thence to Aunt Fannie's home in Buckland. Uncle and Mary Ann came into Bideford about noon with the donkey and cart. I could have ridden with them if I had wanted to, but I preferred riding in the cars with Pa and Ma. It seemed so queer to be packing this morning for it seems only yesterday that we came here, but instead of that it is nearly three weeks.

It was market day today so we walked through the market and Aunt Fannie was in so we rode to Buckland with her in the horse and cart. It was very easy riding, but I should think it was very heavy for the horse for there were seven of us to ride over six miles. Well at last we arrived in sight of Buckland Brewer, a place that Ma has often been in her childhood. It is quite a large place, larger than I expected, but I do not like it as well as I do Instow for it is so far away from the grand old ocean. It is not such a quiet place and there is not river or sea here so I miss them ever so much, but I must retire for it is nearly twelve o'clock.

Devonshire

Buckland Brewer, Wednesday June 8th, 1870

This morning after breakfast we walked over to the graveyard. It is just across the street from here so we did not have very far to go. There were a great many buried there that Ma used to know well when she was young and they are nearly all passed away. This afternoon the ladies' club met here. They meet once a year for tea, in fact it was like a regular fair here. After they gathered the roll was called, then they marched to the chapel with the band, but they did not play well. First it sounded more like boys drumming on tin pans and pails. Ma, Pa and I went to the chapel. The sermon that was preached was very good and appropriate for the occasion. Then they marched with the band through the streets and went to tea at the house near Aunt's. Out in the street were five or six candy and toy stalls and I guess they made considerable for every child must have bought something and I never saw so many children under ten before. And such a noise as they made. It was enough to distract one and almost everyone in the neighborhood seemed to be out, but I did not enjoy myself very much. It was so tiresome.

We went down to cousin Robert's to tea. I like him and his wife very much and they have four sweet children, three girls and one boy. They half atone for my not seeing sister Annie's children. We stayed there to supper which was not until eleven o'clock (the time that all respectable people like us should be in bed) and we did not get home until after midnight. The fair had not broken up yet and did not until daylight, for I expect they enjoyed themselves finely for they were dancing.

Buckland Brewer, Thursday June 9th, 1870

Today the weather is clear and warm and it is real pleasant. Today I am fifteen years old. Won't it be nice to say that I spent my fifteenth birthday at Aunt Fannie's in Buckland Brewer, Devonshire, England. Uncle keeps the Post Office and while we were eating breakfast the postman came. He brought two letters for Ma and two for me. One of Ma's letters was from home. They were all well. The other one was from cousin Thomas. One of mine was from Mary Ann and the other one was from Thomas. He also sent me a little box containing a beautiful pair of gold earrings. He said in his letter he hoped I would please accept them from my 'teasing cousin'. He also said he should drink to my health and wish me a long and happy life. Cousin Ellen presented me with a very large and handsome wax doll and cousin Sarah gave me a nice 'Lady's Companion', furnished nicely and she gave me a real pretty needle book.

Ma sent a letter home this morning and I wrote to Instow to thank Thomas for his present and to answer his kind letter, also to answer the letter that I received from Mary Ann. Just before dinner Pa, Ma, Aunt and myself went to Charlie's. I like his wife very much, she is so pleasant. I think she is so quiet and that is what I like (because you know I am so quiet myself that I could not help liking one of the same disposition). They have four fine healthy children, but I do not think they are as pretty as Robert's children. Two gentlemen and a little boy from Fremington a distance of about twelve miles was there, also cousin Lewis and his wife and children and Robert and his wife so you see we made quite a party altogether and we had a real pleasant time. For dinner we had new potatoes, the first I have had this season. They were quite large and were real good. We stayed to supper and until late evening. For supper we had a junket, but it was not as good as the one we had in Instow. I enjoyed myself a great deal more than I did yesterday, but I never saw such a place as England is for drinking beer and spirits. It is nothing but drink, drink, drink with those that will take it. At every house that we have been they press us to have some beer or wine or gin. I declare it beats everything, but we never took anything, anywhere as we are not in the habit of doing so.

There are not any stoves in England but fire places and boilers are used instead. I do not like either of them as well as I do a stove. After tea we all sat around the open fireplace and had a very pleasant time talking about America etc. About half past eleven we all started back home again. It was real pleasant walking home through the narrow lanes and across the green meadows in the bright moonlight and I enjoyed it very much. I sang the piece entitled, *Once I Was Single*[1] for them and oh! how they did laugh. Tonight we also retired about midnight.

Buckland Brewer, Friday June 10th, 1870

This morning I amused myself by playing dominoes with Pa, Ma and Sarah. After dinner Ellen and myself

1. *Once when I was Single* is a folk song. A few lines of the song are:
"When I was single my shoes they did squeak,
But now I am married my shoes they go leak.
O-o-oh, I wish I was a single girl, O-o-oh, I wish I was a single girl again.
When I was single I dressed very fine,
But now I am married I go ragged all the time.
O-o-oh, I wish I was a single girl, O-o-oh, I wish I was a single girl again..."

went out for a little walk. We went to a lady's garden and saw some beautiful flowers. She also has a very large lemon tree pinned up against the wall. She gave us each a bouquet of roses. They were just lovely for they were such a deep pink and were very large. When we came back Aunt, Ma, Ellen and myself went to Mrs. Tucker's to tea. Ma used to be well acquainted with her before she went to America. She is a very pleasant lady but is also a very great talker. Her husband has been dead several years and she and her servant live alone. We had a very pleasant time with her and returned to Aunts about ten o'clock.

Buckland Brewer, Saturday June 11th, 1870

This morning after breakfast I went over in the church yard or grave yard. Some of the inscriptions on the tomb stones were rather queer. I copied a few of them as follows –

All you, my friends as you pass by,
Behold the spot where I do lie.
From all my grief's and troubles free.
Prepare yourselves to follow me.

Another –
My husband and my children dear,
Remember I was buried here,
My debt is paid - my grave you see,
Prepare yourselves to follow me.

This one was written in the year 1829 -
Praises on tombs are trifles vainly spent,
A man's good name is his own monument.

Another –
Weep not for me my children dear,
I am not dead but sleeping here,

When this you see remember me,
And think on death and follow me.

Another-
Reader one moment stop and think,
That I am in eternity and thou on the brink.'

Some of the graves are very old and I saw several stones dated as far back as the year 1600. After dinner Pa, Ma, Uncle, Auntie and myself went to Cleave Farm where Cousin Lewis lives. His wife is a very fleshy, rosy cheeked woman, but is very pleasant. They have two children. The oldest is a little boy and is a poor sickly little thing but the little girl is fleshy and healthy like her mother. Their place is very quiet and lonely and I think I should get lonesome if I remained there very long. We took tea there and had quite a pleasant time.

Uncle wanted me to sing for them so I sang *Maggie* and *Jamie* and *Once I Was Single.* Of course they laughed considerably at the last piece but I am about tired of the old thing and pretty soon I am almost afraid I shall forget myself and shall think that I am really married. Our walk back to Aunt Fannie's, through the green lanes and across meadows was a very pleasant one and we all enjoyed it very much and I gathered a few very pretty wild flowers from the hedges.

Buckland Brewer, Sunday June 12th, 1870

This morning Pa, Ma, Sarah and myself went to the Bible Christian chapel. We heard a very good sermon preached from Matthew (5th chapter, 13th verse). When we got home cousin Thomas was there and we were very glad to see him. In the afternoon Pa, Ma, Thomas, Ellen, Sarah and myself went to the church across the road. I never heard the English services read before and I like them very much.

Thomas, Ellen, Sarah and myself went walking and I enjoyed myself very much. In the evening Pa, Ma, Thomas and myself went to the Wesleyan chapel. The minister preached from the Ecclesiastes, (8th chapter, 10th verse). After meeting Thomas, Sarah and myself took a short walk. I think Sarah is real pleasant company and I think she looks a little bit like Sister Fannie. Thomas started for Instow about ten o'clock and I sent a letter to Mary Ann by him. After he was gone, Sarah and I went down to Robert's a few minutes.

Buckland Brewer, Monday June 13th, 1870

This morning Uncle took Pa, Ma, Auntie and myself out for a day's ride. The places we visited were those that Ma used to go to in her girlhood, and it was very pleasant to her to visit the old places once more. First we went to Tuckingmill and saw Mr. Jule, a person that Ma used to be well acquainted with. Then we went to Parkham Town[2] where Ma used to attend church. We visited the grave yard and saw Grandmother's [Jane Squance Clement] grave. The inscription on her tombstone was as follows –

A loving virtuous wife and tender parent dear,
A true and faithful friend in dust lies buried here.
Afflicting: is my loss yet why should I complain,
Since her I loved, I trust has found eternal gain.
She died December 8th in the year 1822. Aged 37 years.

The carpenters were repairing the church but we went in and saw the place where Ma and Auntie used to sit. Then Auntie, Ma and myself went up eighty-eight steps

2. Parkham is a village and parish near Bideford. Its population in 1861 was 886.

to the top of the tower. I wrote my name and residence and the date up there. This church was built in the year 1480, just twelve years before beloved America was discovered. The minister was in the church and he gave us a piece of the wood that was used in building it. He gave it to us as a relic to remember the old church of Parkham Town with, where Ma and Auntie were baptized. Then we went to the house where my great-grandmother used to live and where Grandma was born. The house was used as an inn so we ate dinner there. Then Pa went to the ministers and got the date when Ma's stepmother was baptized so as to know how old she is. She was baptized in October 26 in the year 1774. So she will be nearly ninety-six years old now.

After we left Parkham we rode a good many miles and saw a good many places where Ma used to go before she left England. At last we found ourselves out on the moors at Thornhill Head[3] for a tea meeting. These gatherings are something like the picnics we have at home. There were a great many there and everybody seemed to enjoy themselves. The price of tea was six pence a piece or about fifteen cents of American currency. About seven o'clock we got back to Buckland again. Then Pa, Ma, Ellen and myself went over to the church. We went up one hundred and thirty-five steps to the top of the tower. I wrote my name up there too.

The floor of the church is composed of tombstones of the rich and great men of the church. On one of the slabs I saw the date 1184 but I do not think the church looks quite as old as that or 686 years. I played on the

4. The harmonium became popular in the second half of the nineteenth century. The bellows were pumped by two foot pedals and one or two keyboards. It was a popular instrument for churches which could not afford a pipe organ and was a favourite for home music making alongside the piano and organ.

harmonium[4] here and sang the piece entitled *Golden Shore.* Today when we went to Thornhill Head we saw the grave of my great Aunt Fannie.

Buckland Brewer, Tuesday June 14th, 1870

This morning I went over in the graveyard again. Through the yard leading from the gate to the church door, there are two rows of very large trees and I like to go and sit under them. This morning I saw two more queer inscriptions that I wish to write down here as they were on the stone:

Here lie buried in their mothers grave ye bodies of Mrs. Jane and Mrs. Elizabeth Lambe both of this parish.
Mrs. Elizabeth was buried ye 28th of February Anno Domini 1731½ Aetatis 38.
Mrs. Jane was buried ye 8th of November 1732 Aetatis 45.
These sisters lived a Pious Godly life
They Envied none, they strangers were to strife
But Neither of 'em ever was a wife.
These Virgins pure, defied Deaths poisonous sting
Being always fit to meet their Heavenly King
Their whole desires were fixed in Heaven above
With Angels to Enjoy seeaplick love
Forever to remain in perfect Bliss
Consumate Joy, eternal Happiness

The following was written in the year 1807---
Vain world farewell: I've seen enough of thee
I careless am of what thou say'st of me
Thy smiles I never court not frowns did fear
My glass is run, my head rests quiet here
What faults in me, you saw, take care to skun
And look to home --- enough is to be done
I was and am not, ask no more of me
It's all I am and all that thou shalt be.

This morning I cut my name in the church side door with my pen knife, wasn't I naughty? After I got back Sarah and I went to the well after a pitcher of water. The water pitchers are large stone or earthen jugs and they are very heavy. In this part of England the floors of houses in the lowest storey are nearly all stone or slate. In Bideford we saw a sanded floor but I did not like walking on it a bit.

After dinner Pa, Ma, Uncle, Aunt and myself went to Stone Farm, the place where Ma was born. First we went and looked in each field that Grandfather used to own, also the house. A part of the house was destroyed and Ma said everything was very much changed and she could hardly believe it was Stone. The yellow plum trees that used to be pinned up against the house were gone and so was the orchard. Grandmother died in this house and we saw her grave in Parkham Town yesterday. Then we went to the house where Ma's Aunt Mary used to live. We went in the very room where my great grandfather died, also Ma's uncle died.

Our walk back to Auntie's was a very pleasant one through the green lanes and fields and I gathered a few pretty wild flowers and ferns to press. At home we have a few ferns that came from India and now I shall have some that shall go from England. I never saw so many before, along the hedges it is just thick in some places and I never saw so much ivy before, it grows so pretty here. Just opposite from the window from where I sit writing is a stone house, the end of which is completely covered and all up over the chimney too, you would hardly know there was one. But dear me, it beats everything I ever saw to see so many hills and valleys, in fact England is nothing else but hills and valleys and I pity the poor horses, especially when they carry heavy loads.

This part of the country is very hilly and the scenery is lovely, but it is altogether a different thing if a person is obliged to walk very far for just as soon as you get nicely to the foot of a hill, there is another very steep one for you to ascend again, and so on. After tea Ellen and myself went out for a walk. It was so pleasant walking along the cozy little lanes in the moonlight. Some of the lanes are very narrow and just wide enough for two to walk side by side. One lane near here is a very long, narrow and shady one and is very appropriately named 'Lovers Lane'. The lane is just wide enough for two to walk together and in fact the name suits it very nicely.

Buckland Brewer, Wednesday June 15th, 1870

This morning it is very cloudy and gloomy. If we have this weather for many days I believe I shall get homesick. After dinner Ma and myself packed our trunks for tomorrow we are going away from here. Uncle is going to take us over to Christopher Clement's, Ma's cousin. In the afternoon he came over here to invite Aunt to go with us tomorrow. After tea Sarah and myself took a nice long walk. First we went down to Robert's and I enjoyed a few hours there for Ann [Withecombe], cousin Robert's wife tries to make everything so pleasant. Before we left there she asked me to sing, *Once I Was Single* and I complied with her request.

Today a man was talking with me about America and among other questions he had the impudence to ask if "there were any wise people" living out here. I did not like this question very well and told him that as a general rule I thought the people in America were much wiser then in England. This same ignorant person also asked if "America was a village or a city". The idea of America or the United States with its thirty-seven states and nine territories, besides the large extent of country both north and south, the very idea of all this being called a little village seemed to me rather foolish and it took some time to answer him. I could not make him believe that just the state of Illinois is nearly as large as all England.

Some think that nothing grows in our country and that the inhabitants are a barbarous race of people, and that the climate of the country is either hot enough to roast or is cold enough to freeze. Well I just wish a few of the ignorant ones would visit America and find out all about it for themselves for if they do not they will never believe that a greater abundance and variety of everything grows there than in England and that the greater part of the inhabitants are not savage, but a civilized nation. They will also find that our climate is neither hot enough to roast or cold enough to freeze people often.

Buckland Brewer, Thursday June 16th, 1870

This morning Uncle took Pa, Ma, Aunt and myself over to Christopher [Clement], Gillscot Farm, Alwington Parish[5]. We had a very pleasant ride but were continually going up and down hills. Some of the hills were several hundred feet high so we were obliged to drive slow and it took us about an hour to travel the three miles. Mrs. Clement is a very pleasant little woman and tried to make us feel at home. Mr. Clement's sister [Catherine Clement] lives with them. She is an old maid about fifty-nine years old. She is so very fleshy that she can hardly walk. There are no children here so it will be nice and quiet. The sea is just a little way from here so I shall go down to the beach quite often I expect.

5. Alwington is a small parish near Bideford. In 1844 it had 392 inhabitants. The church is dedicated to St. Andrew with a fine old stone building and tower. There is also a Wesleyan chapel.

After dinner Pa, Ma, Auntie and myself went down to look at the sea. We had to go down over a very steep hill and just at the foot of this hill the tide comes roaring and splashing against the Pebble Ridge. The tide was coming in and it was just grand. I could watch it for hours and not get tired. We picked a few limpets off the rocks. They are a small shellfish that cling very tight to the rocks and unless you knock them off with the first blow you cannot get them off at all. I have often heard the expression 'cling so tight as a limpet to a rock' but I could never fully comprehend its meaning before. We enjoyed ourselves down by the water very much but it was not very pleasant going back to Mr. Clement's up over that steep hill and we were obliged to sit down and rest ever so many times before we arrived at the top. It made Aunt sick and she could scarcely get to the house. She is not very healthy anyway.

After tea Uncle and Aunt went back to Buckland Brewer again. Soon after they left it commenced to rain and it made everything look so fresh and green. While it was raining I went upstairs and sat down in the large front window and read. Just outside the window, climbing up against the house, there is a large sweet briar bush and the rain did make it smell so sweet. The rain was very welcome to all of the farmers around here for everything in the garden and fields are dying for the want of water. This house was built in the year 1831. The date is cut in the large stone chimney. John Clement, Christopher's brother, cut it there before he moved to Canada. We ate supper about nine o'clock, and I did not remain up very long after that for I was rather tired and I had a severe headache.

Gillscot Farm, Alwington Parish, Friday June 17th, 1870

This morning it is raining again and it is very wet and disagreeable out doors. About nine o'clock Pa went to the Post Office and got a letter from home. They were all well. The night that they wrote, the sociable met at our house and I should like to have been there. It seems to me, it must have seemed rather strange to sister Fannie to have three such important persons as Pa, Ma and Lute[6] absent. After dinner Mrs. Clement, Pa, Ma and myself walked over to Peppercombe, a little place by the sea, a little way from Gillscot farm. The ridge extends along by the sea there too and I picked up a few pretty pebbles. One of them was just the size and shape of an egg, and I shall take it home. We saw the ruins of a limekiln where Grandfather used to get lime. Then we visited a lady's flower and fruit garden. There was a large variety of beautiful flowers and the fruit was very fine. We saw pears, peaches, and figs growing. I never saw a fig tree before. Our walk back was very pleasant.

Gillscot Farm, Saturday June 18th, 1870

This morning it is raining again and is quite cold. Until dinner time I amused myself by reading from a book entitled, *Uncle Tom's Cabin.*[7] After dinner I went out in the garden and I had a pleasant time for there are so many nice shady places. In the front yard on each side of the path from the gate to the house there is a nice row of white thorn trees, all cut low and trimmed off even and they do look very pretty. Pa says he would give a thousand dollars if we had a row just like them each side of our walk at home. I should like to take a

6. 'Lute' was Lucy's family nickname

7. *Uncle Tom's Cabin,* a novel by Harriet Beecher Stowe, was first published in 1852. It is credited with inflaming the Northern states to work towards the abolition of slavery which eventually led to the American Civil War.

peep into a certain brick house of Rockford this morning, very much, but then they are not up yet (the lazy things) for it is about ten here so we will be in bed sound asleep when they will be up.

After dinner Pa, Ma, and myself had another walk down over that steep hill to the sea again. At this place it is called Portledge Mouth. We had a nice long ramble all over the rocks and cliffs and sands and I picked up a few pretty shells and pebbles. We saw several poor women picking limpets to sell and to fatten their ducks with. Then we saw a man hauling sand with a horse and sand bags. We enjoyed ourselves down on the beach very much.

Gillscot Farm, Sunday June 19th, 1870

This morning Pa did not feel very well so he remained with Mrs. Clement and Catherine while Mr. Clement, Ma and myself went to Alwington church. It was a real pretty neat little church about two miles from Gillscot. The sermon was a very good one taken from Deuteronomy (7th chapter, 6th verse). After dinner I took a book and went out on a high hill overlooking the sea and had a nice time reading.

At six o'clock Mrs. Clement, Ma and myself went to Holwell chapel. The text was taken from Luke (14th chapter, 16th verse). I like Mrs. Clement very much. She is a quiet person but is very pleasant. Ma and her used to be playmates. Our walk home was very pleasant. The sun was just setting over Lundy Island[8] and it did look so bright and nice. After we got back I went out on the hills again and read until nearly dark. It was

8. Lundy Island rises approximately 400 feet out of the Bristol Channel about 11 miles off the North Devon coast. It is a granite outcrop about three miles long and half a mile wide.

real pleasant up on the hills and I enjoyed myself very much.

Gillscot Farm, Monday June 20th, 1870

This morning it is very cloudy and gloomy and it makes me feel gloomy too. I must say I never felt so stupid before. I guess I must have caught cold yesterday when I went to sleep out doors. And then this morning after breakfast, I went to sleep up in my room by the window with the wind blowing right on me and so, I suppose, all of it together caused this indescribable stupidity. This afternoon Ma, Pa, Miss Catherine Clement and I went over to a cousin of Ma's to spend the afternoon and take tea with them. Mr. and Mrs. Lane were very pleasant people and we enjoyed ourselves there very much. They have a very nice garden, such a large assortment of flowers, then the fruit was nice too. The cherries were ripe and they were just splendid. I like their garden, there were so many nice little shady nooks and corners. Mrs. Lane made us each a glass of metheglin. It is a nice cool drink made of water, honey and spice etc. Miss Clement has a large assortment of flowers and they are very pretty. She is 59 years old and very fleshy and very odd too. We have new potatoes for supper, but it is not the first I have had for we had them at Cousin Charles' on my birthday, June 9.

We enjoyed ourselves very much indeed and they were very kind and tried to make it as pleasant as possible. We started for home about nine and one-half o'clock and we had a very pleasant walk back in the cool of the evening. We did not go through the fields again but around by the road so we did not have quite so many steep hills to climb. As soon as we got home I retired directly and was very soon in the Land of Nod, dreaming of my dear friends and relative at home.

Gillscot Farm, Tuesday June 21st, 1870

This morning it was clear and bright, such a contrast from what it was yesterday morning. About ten o'clock Pa, Ma and myself rode to Bideford with Mr. Clement. It is about four miles from Gillscot farm. We got to Bideford about eleven o'clock. We wanted to go to Instow but the train had just left for there, and the next one did not leave for two hours so Pa went down to the wharf and hired a man to row us down the river. It took the man about an hour to row us down the three miles. We had a very pleasant ride and I enjoyed myself ever so much.

Our friends in Instow did not expect us so we gave them a pleasant surprise. We remained to Uncle John's [Rodd] to dinner then went back to Bideford by the four o'clock train. It was market day there so we went through the market house and saw Cousin Robert [Withecombe] and Martha and Charlie's wife, also Ellen [Withecombe]. About five o'clock we went to the hotel where Mr. Clement stops and found him waiting for us, and soon we started and had a nice ride back to Gillscot. The people in this part of England pronounce 'either' as if it was spelled 'ither' and it sounds so queer to me. After tea I had a nice time reading from a very old book. There were a few queer inscriptions in it that I wish to copy here. I shall spell the words just as they were in the book as follows:

Edwards Yarde of Clist Honiton.
Who ever wants a rule his life to scan
Lo! here's ye mete yard of an honest man
Much time he spent in heavenly contemplation
In sacred studyes, prayers and mediations.
The Saintes Socitety he did most dearly love
and a true friend to Saintes himself did prove
He took ye Churches case to hart –

he grieved at Gods dishonour –
He ye poor relieved
He, Abraham- like instructed oft his own and Moses-like,
a peacefulman was known
Harmless and prideless—careless of earths pelf
A friend to learning—courtesy itself.

The date and age of this inscription is now quite obliterated if ever inserted but must have been written more that two hundred and fifty years ago as the one that copied it from the tombstone died in the year 1640. The following is on the tombstone of Abraham Barnfield of Langtree who died in 1688:

Out of Gods Field into His barn are gone
They, who whilst here, were Barn and Field in our
Heaven's Gods Barn, ye World here is His Field--
This latter, Tares as well as Wheat doth yield.
But in Gods Barn, nought but the Wheat shall be
In Joy and bliss to all eternity.

Here is one from near Exeter:
There sleeps below; William Stuart
Professor of Sacred Theology
The greatest of Sinners.

Formerly Fellow of the College of St John the Baptist Oxo Lately,
Rector of this Parish and Chancellor of this Dio
Now, Dust and Ashes.
And whatsoever else is really unreal.
On the 12th day of the month of September in the year 1734.
This least of Penitents restored his soul to a propitious duty.

The following is in memory of the Bamplylde family near Barnstaple:

Stand passenger; gaze, such was he
As thou, tremble, such shalt thou be
He dyed to live, so live to dye
Depart; muse on eternity.

The following is in memory of John Rosier died in 1685:

Lo! with a warrant sealed by Gods decree
Death his grim segriant hatth arrested me
No bayle was to be given, no law could save
My body from the prison of the Grave
Yet by the Gospell my poore soule had got
A supersedeas and Death seazed it not
And for my downe cast body here it lyes
A prisoner of hope it shall rise
Faith noth assure me, God of his great love
In Christ will send a writt for my remove
And set my body my soule is free
With Christ-in-heaven—Come glorious liberatie

The following epigram is found on the Abbey Church at Bath on Bishop Shuttleworth:

These walls so full of monument and bust
Show how Bath waters serve to lay the dust.

Here is a Countesbury church-wardens account for 1687:

	£	s	d
Payd when I took my office at barnstapel	*0*	*1*	*6*
Payd for glasing ye belfery and church windows		*2*	*0*
" ye 8th Sept. to one Souldyyer, for releife	*0*	*1*	*0*
Layd out to a petition to hannah harris			
To redeem her husband turkey	*0*	*0*	*6*
Payd John Streat for killing two grays [badgers]	*0*	*1*	*0*
" Jasper Kiddy for righting ye bel whels & nayles		*0*	*4*
Payd for wishing ye surpls	*0*	*0*	*6*

" for new herse cloth and new table cloth for ye Chancel bord	*1 9 3*
Payd for bread and wine for communion At Easter	*10 2*
Payd ye Fox Catcher for taking foxes on yeere	*15 0*
Total	*2 2 3*

Gillscot Farm, Wednesday, June 22nd, 1870

The other day I said something I want to take back. I said the young gents were not very gentlemanly, but there was one here last night that almost overdid himself with politeness. This morning about ten o'clock Pa, Ma and myself bid farewell to Mr. and Mrs. Clement and Catherine and went to visit some of Ma's acquaintance's. I took Grandfather's picture and went up to Mrs. Lane's to show it to her and met Pa and Ma at Horns Cross and then we walked on to Broadparkham together to see Mrs. Betsy Kivell, a cousin to the Kivells in Canada. She a very queer old fashioned woman and talks real funny though I suppose she could not help it. I think she is a great flatterer. When Ma told her who I was, she exclaimed: "Dear me, Mrs. Rodd, what a beautiful little daughter you have but she looks so tired, the dear little honey."

We did not have dinner until about three o'clock for she said she wanted to keep us with her just as long as possible, but still she was not in the room with us half of the time. I did not enjoy my dinner very much although I was rather hungry, for the vegetables did not seem to be more than half cooked. When we left there we called on several persons that Ma used to know before she left England, then we went to Newhaven where Mr. Clement's hired man met us with the horse and trap and drove us to Buckland Brewer to Aunt Fannie's. Our friends there seemed pleased to welcome us back again and we were very glad to see them all once more. After tea Ma and myself went up to Stone. We saw the person that lives there and she gave us permission to dig up a few lent-lily[10] roots from the orchard hedge of the house where Ma was born. Ma says the lent-lily is a beautiful yellow flower that blossoms in Lent. The ground was very dry and hard so it took us a long time to get any roots but we managed to dig up about a dozen and then we had a nice little walk. I picked a few very pretty wild flowers and a few fern leaves.

On top of the barn up to Higher Stone farm there is a weather cock with a date 1718 on it. After we returned, I went out walking again with Cousin Sarah. We went down to Robert's a few minutes and I bid them good bye for tomorrow we leave here and go down in Cornwall to visit a few friends. We had a very pleasant walk and I suppose it is the last time we will ever walk together.

Buckland Brewer, Thursday June 23rd, 1870

All the morning Ma and myself were engaged in repacking our trunks. Just before dinner the postman came but had nothing for <u>us</u>. He said the postman at Gillscot had a letter for us so Cousin Lewis took the pony and went after it.

When he got to Gillscot he found that the letter had been taken to another place but he went after it and got back to Buckland Brewer just as we were ready to start. Uncle Withecombe took us about two and a half miles to Catsberry Gate to meet the coach. I guess after a while I shall get used to meeting and parting with our dear friends. It seemed almost like leaving home. Aunt felt it a good deal to part from her sister and in fact we all

10. Lent-lily is another name for a daffodil.

felt badly. Ma is 1½ years older than Aunt Fannie, but looks that much younger in my opinion. I should not wonder if we see Ellen and Sarah out to Rockford some of these days for they both want to go very much and Ellen's intended wants to go too.

After a while the coach came to take us and our luggage on board and away we were again. The coach was a nice large one and would seat about twenty persons. It required three horses to draw it and we changed horses and stopped for refreshments halfway between Bideford and Holsworthy. The scenery part of the way was just lovely. We passed through a great deal of moory land [Bodmin Moor] and some places made us think of the prairies at home. We passed along by several canals and saw the horses walking along by the side of them and drawing the boat of stone etc. up and down the canals.

About five o'clock we arrived in Holsworthy[11] where Uncle Richard Gerry and cousin Fannie Rodd met us. We did not expect to see them for Uncle lives in Pyworthy so they gave us a very pleasant surprise. Cousin Fannie has been living with Uncle [Richard] Gerry since Aunt Mary[12] died. We all went to a hotel and Pa ordered supper for all of us which I ate with a relish, then we went out for a little walk around the place. Holsworthy is quite a large place and there are several fine buildings there. The Market house was a nice large building. We went in the Methodist chapel. It is a new structure and a very fine one. Pa used to come to Holsworthy often before he left England and he says the place looked quite

11. Holsworthy is mentioned in the Domesday survey of 1086. The National Gazetteer of Great Britain and Ireland of 1868 describes it as a small market town with a population of 1,857.
12. Aunt Mary Gerry was Lucy's father's sister who had died days before they arrived in England.

natural. Pa and Ma remained at the hotel over night and I went home with Uncle to Pyworthy[13] although I could have stayed with Pa and Ma at the hotel if I had wanted to, but I thought I would like to take a ride behind that little pony of theirs. Fannie and I went to a neighbor to stay all night for Uncle's house is not a very large one. Uncle lives about four miles from Holsworthy

Pyworthy, Friday June 24th, 1870

Today it is mid-summer day. First this morning it rained quite hard then the sun shone out and it was real warm. About nine o'clock Uncle and myself went to Holsworthy. We found Pa and Ma quite well. We all visited the graveyard and went in the church. It was a very neat little church but not as pretty as Alwington church. We went up ninety steps to the top of the tower. The scenery was grand and we could see so far each way. When we were going up, the bells tolled and the clock struck. They made such an awful noise, it almost deafened us. It was St John's day and when we got down they were reading the Episcopal services so were obliged to remain in the belfry nearly an hour. Was not that a pretty good joke! We found it a little too good for we got oh so tired.

Well at last we were at liberty to go. We went to the hotel and got our things then Uncle took us to his house. We went around by Pa's birthplace. The house was nearly gone to rack and ruin. Pa showed me the play-grounds where he used to play. The window panes of the house were nearly all broke. I took a little stone and broke a little piece of glass out, and shall take it home to remember the old place with. In a house near

13. Pyworthy is a parish two miles south of Holsworthy in Devon and borders Cornwall. The 1870 Pyworthy Commercial Directory and Gazetteer Trades and Professions lists Richard Gerry as a farmer of East Yeomadon.

Pa's birth place we saw three men that used to be boys when Pa was and they used to play together.

We arrived at Uncle's at about two o'clock where we ate a very hearty meal, for our long ride had given us a good appetite. Uncle Gerry married Pa's sister Mary, the one that died the day before we landed in Liverpool, and cousin Fannie Rodd has been staying with Uncle a few weeks, but now he has a housekeeper so Fannie is going home to Instow next week. After dinner Ma, Fannie and myself had a nice walk in the garden then we went down in the lanes and gathered a few wild strawberries from the hedges. After tea Pa, Ma, Fannie and myself rode to Pyworthy. It is about one mile from Uncle's. We visited the churchyard [St Swithin's Church] and saw the graves of Grandpa, Grandma and Aunt Mary. Pa is going to have a tombstone erected in memory of them. We went into the church. I think it must be pretty old for the walls are beginning to decay. We wanted to go up in the tower but could not for the belfry was locked. Then we went to see several persons that Pa used to be well acquainted with before he went to America and they were all very glad to see him once more.

Pyworthy, Saturday June 25th, 1870

This morning we did not get up until about seven o'clock for we have not been to bed until late for several nights and in fact not since we left our beloved Rockford. Before we left Uncle's, he gave me Aunt Mary's bible that she had had since 1845, 25 years ago, and I am going to try and get the date of her birth and death and write it in. About eleven o'clock Pa, Ma, Uncle, cousin Fannie and myself started for Joseph Clement's, Ma's cousin. On our way we saw some very pretty places, but still I had much rather, live in the brick house on the corner in the city of Rockford.

We arrived at his house at about two o'clock and they seemed very glad to see us. After we had had lunch, Fannie and I wandered all over the gardens and orchard and enjoyed ourselves finely, at least I did and I rather guess she did too, as she is nine years older than I am, but there is one consolation and that is she is but a very little taller than I. I think I shall like it here, for I shall be able to read and write all I like for there are not children younger then twenty-five to interrupt or disturb me. About six o'clock Uncle and Fannie started for home again, but left us three to spend a few days here and then we expect to go to Launceston to see Pa's brothers. After they were gone I amused myself by reading and writing. Well, I have taken my tea (or rather hot water, for I have not tasted a drop of tea or coffee since I left home) and here I sit out in the green meadow writing in my journal, with the calves standing near watching me with wondering eyes and with the cry of rooks in the rookery near by. It was really amusing to hear them chattering so to each other. Now is that not a very pleasant situation? I think it is and I enjoy it finely but I must close and go in doors for the dew is falling fast.

Stowford Farm, Halwill, Sunday June 26th, 1870

Time passes on and still another Sunday has rolled around. Neither of us did go to church this morning for the church is two miles away and Pa was lame and Ma and I did not feel disposed to walk that far and in fact we were all lame or stiff which is the effect of going up in Holsworthy tower on Friday, so I was reading all morning. After dinner Pa, Ma, Mr. and Miss Clement rode to chapel, but I did not care about going. After they were gone, I took my book and started for the orchard and in my travels I found a dear little kitten, so I took it up and went on my way rejoicing, but in vain were my efforts to keep it for it was 'as slippery as an eel' so I finished my journey without it and went to writing instead of reading. So here I sit on the limb of a fallen apple tree, writing in my journal and as I have nothing much to say, I will speak of Mr. and Mrs. Clement and family. First of course comes Mr. Clement. He is a tall and elderly person of about 60, not bad looking, though of course he couldn't be as he is a cousin of Ma's. His wife looks older then he is for she has more gray hairs in her head and she is very good looking also, for her hair is wavy. They have four or five boys and three or four girls. Christopher is the youngest and is very good looking. He is a preacher, but has not been able to preach for some time on account of sickness and he has not been able to read either so (as he said) to keep his hands from idleness, he has made several tidies and lamp mats and he has knit several pairs of mittens. Now just think of that and aren't I glad he is my second cousin, but I must go in doors for it is quite chilly and Ma would say "Well now, have not you got more sense then that" so I will show I have got more sense than to stay out here long. Well, after I went in the house I amused myself by reading some nice long pieces from a book, *Sunday at Home*.[13]

I wonder what they are doing at home now. I suppose that the morning services are not over yet, for it cannot be more then half past eleven. I wonder who remains at home to take care of the house and how Annie and William and their little family are, what are they saying about us, but there I should wonder all day. I should not

13. *Sunday at Home* by Nathanial Hawthorne begins: "Every Sabbath morning, in the summer time, I thrust back the curtain, to watch the sunrise stealing down a steeple, which stands opposite my chamber window. First, the weathercock begins to flash; then, a fainter lustre gives the spire an airy aspect; next it encroaches on the tower, and causes the index of the dial to glisten like gold, as it points to the gilded figure of the hour...."

be able to find out, so I may as well quit wondering for I am going to read again, until Pa, Ma and the rest return for then I shall want them to tell me about the anniversary if it was held this afternoon, although I guess it will be held this evening and tomorrow afternoon. There will be a tea meeting at twelve pence each or about twenty-eight cents in American money and they have very good teas too or least they did up at Thornhill Head on Monday the 13th of this month. When Ma came home she said she was glad that I did not go for it was so very cold and so am I for I have a cold already. Neither of us went to the meeting this evening. I read aloud to them from Sunday at Home until after ten o'clock and then we retired and soon after I entered the Land of Nod and dreaming of my dear friends and relations at home and in fact dreaming that I was there with them.

Stowford Farm, Monday June 27th, 1870

Today the sun shines out bright and warm. All of the morning I was engaged in reading again for I find plenty of books and papers of every description to suit my taste. Just before dinner a lady friend of Christopher's came and she is going to the tea with us. She is very pleasant person and I like her very much. About three o'clock we all set off in the trap. The trap rides very easy, more so then any I have rode in before. It was almost like riding in one carriage and in fact they call this a carriage. We arrived at the chapel in time for the services which was conducted by a lady and she preached very well too, but I do not think a lady's voice is at all adapted to preaching for it is not strong enough, but this person did well because it was not a very large chapel. After preaching, tea was held down to the school room under the chapel. I enjoyed the tea very much indeed, I think rather more then I did at Thornhill Head, but then that was held out of doors in the hot sun and this was not, so there is a difference. The tea was for the benefit of the chapel, that is, to help pay off the debt that remains on it and I think they took in about eleven pounds (money not weight) or about sixty-six dollars. After tea there were speaking and other exercises again in the chapel, and I liked them all very much. Three gentlemen spoke, then the lady that preached this afternoon spoke a few words and I liked her better than I did the men although she did not speak as long. The services were closed at about half past nine so it was after ten before we arrived at home. I enjoyed our ride back in the moonlight very much indeed and I was very tired.

Stowford Farm, Tuesday June 28th, 1870

This morning I awoke very much refreshed. The sun shines very brightly and I think it will be a very warm day. After breakfast Christopher took his lady-love home. Pa and Ma went out for a walk so I put on my cape (for it was colder than I thought it was) and took a book and went out in the meadow under a large spreading beech tree and there sat down to read and to write away a few hours. The hours did pass away quickly sure enough, for before I was aware of it the dinner hour arrived and I heard Ma calling me so I had to jump up and get ready in a hurry.

After dinner I came out again and here I sit, writing in another shady spot. I am thinking if I should stay at Stowford farm long I should have more then one or two or even three 'sanctums.' The place where I am sitting now is up on an embankment and shaded by large trees. I picked a few wild flowers to press. I must send a few of them to Cousin Dillie for this is her Uncle's farm. After a while Elizabeth came out with a tidy and showed me how to make it so nearly all of the rest of the afternoon I was working on that and in the evening she showed

The view from the railway station at Instow, North Devon, 1890

The Pebble Ridge at Westward Ho! Devon 1875

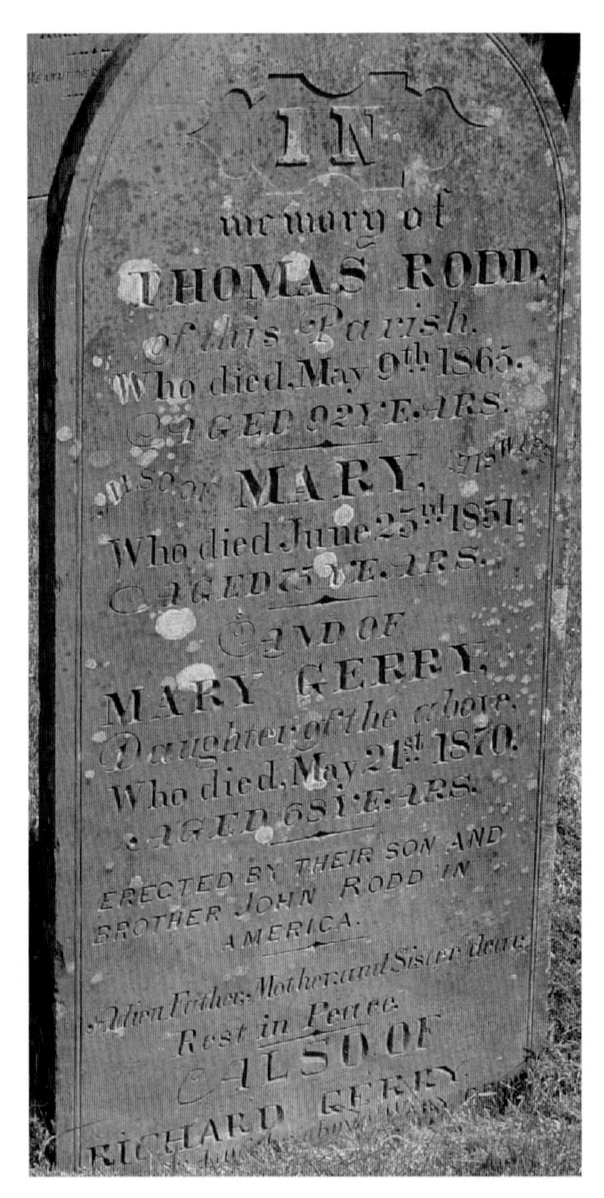

The tombstone of Lucy's grandparents, Thomas and Mary Rodd and her Aunt Mary Gerry, erected by her father at Pyworthy, Devon, in 1870

The path leading up to the top of Launceston Castle,
visited by Lucy in June 1870

Polperro harbour, viewed from the Warren in 1870

Charlotte ('Lottie') Giles (born 1855), daughter of John and Emma Giles of Polperro. This photograph of Lottie by Lewis Harding was taken before Lucy's visit in 1870

me how to net, so tomorrow when we go to Launceston, I shall get a mesh and needle, but I must retire as it is getting late. Good night.

Stowford, Wednesday June 29th, 1870

Well, we had to pack again this morning and it seemed so very queer and then almost as we say "how do you do' to anyone, we must say 'good bye" and I do not like it very much. At about ten and one-half o'clock we said "good bye" to Stowford and the inhabitants and started for Launceston in Cornwall where Uncle Richard [Rodd] lives. Mr. Clement took us there, about ten miles from Stowford, and we arrived there at about two o'clock.

Launceston[14] is a very pretty place and quite a large place too. Uncle Richard looks a little like Pa but not, I think, as much Uncle John does. Aunt is a very little person and quite good looking. She is Uncle [Richard] Gerry's sister so you see that brother and sister married a brother and sister. They have no children so it shall be very quiet here too. I had rather have it so too. After dinner Ma and myself went out in the garden to see the flowers. There was quite a variety of them and they were very pretty. The garden was up as high as the top of the house and it seemed so queer. Mr. Clement started for Stowford farm about four o'clock in the afternoon. Fannie is coming on the morrow and she said she was coming real early.

14. Launceston was the ancient capital of Cornwall. It has been noted for many centuries for its several impressive arch bridges, all which date back to the 15th century or earlier. This ancient town guarded the gateway to Cornwall in medieval times, being on the main northern route into the country. The South Gate of the eleventh century Norman castle still survives.

Cornwall

Launceston, Cornwall, Thursday June 30, 1870

This morning about ten o'clock cousin Fannie Rodd came here from Pyworthy. She is going to stay until Saturday afternoon and I expect we will have a splendid time. About eleven o'clock Pa, Ma, Fannie and myself had a nice walk to Werrington Park. It is the occasional abode of the Duke of Northumberland, situated about two miles from Uncle's. We passed through the pretty villages of Newport and St. Stephen to go to it. The park contains over one hundreds acres all nicely shaded with very large beech, chestnut, and other trees. We saw several hundred deer there. Some of them were dark, some light while others were spotted. We saw both old and young ones and some of them were quite tame. The house was a very large one built of cut stone. I should like to have gone into it. The gardens were laid out beautifully. The fish pond and summer-house was splendid. Near the house there were large fruit trees pinned up against the walls. At the entrance of gentlemen's parks there is a house called a lodge in which the gatekeepers live and no one is allowed to pass into the park unless this person opens the gate for them. After roaming all over the park and getting ourselves pretty well tired out we went back to Uncle's.

After dinner Fannie and myself went up on Windmill Hill. It is the highest hill around here and the scenery from there was grand. Launceston showed itself off to very good advantage. The castle and church could be seen very plainly. After we had viewed the surrounding country to our entire satisfaction we sat down in the shade and had a nice little talk and I enjoyed it ever so much. After tea Pa, Ma, Fannie and myself visited the grand old castle or fortress.[1] The ruins of this ancient fortress are extensive and very interesting. The elevated site on which they stand, partly raised by natural and partly by artificial means, render the present broken and dilapidated portions very prominent objects for a considerable distance around. It is nearly overhung with ivy and has a highly picturesque appearance. The fortress was built more than nine hundred years ago and had partly decayed and fallen away. It is thought it was fortified by the Romans. From the account of Borlase, 'The whole keep is ninety three feet in diameter'. It consisted of three wards. The wall of the first was nearly three feet thick and was used as a parapet for soldiers to fight from and defend the brow of the hill. Six feet within it stands the second wall which is twelve feet thick and has a staircase three feet wide on the left of the entrance, running up to the top of the rampart, the entrance of this staircase has a round arch of stone over it. Passing on to the left, you find the entrance into the innermost ward, and on the left of that entrance, a winding staircase conducts you to the top of the innermost rampart, the wall of which is ten feet thick and thirty two feet high from the floor. The inner room is eighteen feet and six inches in diameter and was divided by a planking into two rooms.

1. Launceston Castle probably dates back as early as 1067. The original Norman motte and bailey castle guarded the main route into Cornwall. By 1650 the castle was in ruins, with only the north gatehouse considered habitable. This was partially demolished in 1764 to provide stone for an impressive new house. The gaol, the last remaining building in the castle grounds, was demolished and the Duke of Northumberland had the castle landscaped and turned into a public park and garden.

The Duke of Northumberland, within the last few years, has very much improved the environs of the castle by putting down the old gaol, and enclosing and planting the mound with shrubbery and a great variety of beautiful flowers, also laying out walks, and tending generally to preserve these interesting and magnificent ruins. The commanding position of the castle gave it such strength and security in ancient times, that many religious houses were established by the monks within its protective precincts. We went up to the top of both outer and inner ramparts and the scenery from there was lovely. We did not remain up there very long for the walls are getting very weak and dangerous. We went up one hundred and fifty five steps. We had a delightful walk through the gardens or Castle Green and then went back to Uncle's.

Launceston town was formerly surrounded by a stone wall having three formidable gates, one of which is now standing. We are obliged to pass though this gate to go to Uncle Richard's. It is called the South Gate.[2] Over this gateway is the jail or calaboose. We saw a boy and girl up there. They were accused of stealing apples, from a gentleman's garden. We did not get home until nearly ten o'clock. I think if I had to live in England I should want to live either in Launceston or Instow for they both appear to be such healthy places.

Launceston, Friday July 1st, 1870

This morning Pa, Ma, Fannie and myself went to see the church. It was erected in the year 1540, on the site of a decayed Catholic chapel in which the priests used to sing mass. It is dedicated to St. Mary Magdalen and

2. Launceston is the only Cornish town to have had a town wall; the only remaining town gate is the 14th century South Gate, at one time used as the town prison.

is a very handsome structure built in the later style of English architecture. The body is built with square blocks of granite covered with a profusion of grotesque and curious ornaments and continued around the whole building by a single letter on each stone, carved within a shield. The tower standing at the west end is formed of different materials and is apparently of much older date. There is a large sun dial on it.

The interior of the church is rich in ornamental carved work, and stately and interesting monuments. The windows were of stained-glass. The figurines represented pictures of the bible in very deep and beautiful colors. One of the windows cost one hundred and fifty pounds or about eight hundred and fifty dollars in American currency. When this church was built, the laborers worked for one penny of English money a day. I played on the harmonium here and sang the *Golden Shore* and *Fannie* and I sang *Shall We Gather At The River*. Then we walked though the graveyard, and the oldest date I could find on the tombstones was 1602.

Then we went around by the depot and back through the town where we bought several views and I thought they were very natural. One was of Werrington Park, another of the Eagle house, a view of Launceston town, one of the South Gate, the interior and exterior of the church and a view of the castle and gardens. After dinner we had a delightful walk up around the new road. It is on the high hill and commands an extensive view of Launceston town and of the surrounding country. We pass the Union or Workhouse.[3] It was a very large building and every thing looked neat and clean around it. This afternoon we received a long letter from home.

3. The Launceston Poor Law Union was built in 1838 to accommodate 150 inmates.

They were all quite well. In the evening Fannie and myself had a pleasant walk down town. All of the shops and stores they have large blinds, and they shut them up and bar them every night. It looks odd to me for at home they do not do so.

Launceston Saturday July 2nd, 1870

This morning it was very cloudy but it did not rain any. After breakfast Pa, Ma, Fannie and myself went down to the market. The market house was built in the year 1844. The display of strawberries, gooseberries and cherries was very fine. The strawberries were six pence a quart or about fourteen cents. The cherries were four pence a pound or about ten cents. Pa thought the market all through was a little better then Bideford market. Then we went to the stone cutters and Pa ordered a tombstone to be sent to Pyworthy graveyard. These are the words to be put on the stone:

In memory of Thomas Rodd of this parish
Who died May 9th, 1865; Aged 92 years.
Also of Mary his wife, who died June 23rd, 1851; Aged 75 years
And of Mary Gerry daughter of the above, who died May 21st, 1870; Aged 68 years.
Erected by their son and brother -
Joseph Rodd in America.[4]
Adieu father, mother and sister dear, rest in peace.

Just before dinner, Uncle William [Rodd], Pa's eldest brother came to see us. I think he is about seventy years old. He and Pa do not look very much alike but still there is a family resemblance. After dinner Aunt and

4. The tombstone had been incorrectly engraved with the name 'John Rodd in America'. Lucy's Uncle Richard Gerry was later buried in the family grave in 1880 at the age of 80.

one of her daughters came also. In the afternoon a lady [Mrs. Eastcott] came here to see Pa. She has an Aunt living in Minnesota and is going to send her little girl [Annie Eastcott] out to her and she wants Pa to take care of her as far as we go. If she does go with us, she will be nice company for me.

Uncle William and wife, and Pa, Ma and myself went to Cousin Margaret's to tea. She has not been married very long but they have a nice little place and we had a good tea there. While we were gone, Fannie went back to Uncle Gerry's at Pyworthy again.

Launceston, Sunday July 3rd, 1870

Today also it was very cloudy but did rain until evening. This morning Pa and Ma went to church, and I commenced a long letter to Emma Johns.[5] After dinner I finished it and took it to the Post Office. Ma wrote to brother Thomas [Johns] and I printed a little note to Frankie [Kyle] and Ella and Freddie [Johns][6] and put it in the same. Ma also wrote to Mr. [Richard] Congdon[7] at Polperro to inform him that we expect to reach that place next Tuesday. In the evening it rained quite hard so we did not go out.

Launceston, Monday July 4th, 1870.

This morning it was very foggy and gloomy and we did not go anywhere. In the afternoon Ma, Auntie and myself went down town. Auntie bought me a real pretty little girl's basket with a view of the Crystal Palace in the bottom of it for a keep-sake. Then we visited the

5. Emma Johns, friend of Lucy and daughter of Richard and Jane [neé Hocken] Johns of Rockford, Illinois.
6. Ella and Freddie Johns, Lucy's niece and nephew, children of William and Ann [neé Rodd] Johns of Rockford. Illinois.
7. Richard Congdon's son, Thomas, was a family friend and minister in Rockford, Illinois, married to Emma [neé Giles].

Wesleyan Cemetery. In the evening Uncle wanted me to sing for him so I sang *Maggie* and *Jamie* and *Home Delights* and *Little Nell.*

Launceston, Tuesday July 5th, 1870.

It rained very hard this morning but not hard enough to prevent us from going, for about eight o'clock the bus came to take us to the depot, so we bid 'farewell' to Uncle and Aunt and were soon seated in the cars bound for Liskeard. Our ride from Launceston to Liskeard was a very pleasant one. The scenery was lovely. Such hills and dales I never saw before. Sometimes on one side of us there was a high hill several hundred feet high, and on the other side there was a pretty little valley far below us. We passed through several long dark tunnels and that was not very pleasant for they do not light the lamps in the cars. We passed through several very large places, among them was Plymouth. Here an excursion party got on the train.

We arrived in Liskeard about eleven o'clock. Mr. Congdon met us there at the station and he appeared very glad to see us. We went to a hotel and had dinner then went out for a little walk to see the place. Liskeard is built on the declivity of a rocky hill with a principal portion of it in a valley. It claims to be one of the oldest towns in the county and like many kindred ones was anciently over-awed by a formidable castle of which at present scarcely any traces remain. Its site is now planted with trees and is used as a public promenade. The parish church is situated on an eminence on the eastern side of town and is dedicated to St. Martin. Within the church are several very interesting monuments. A large and handsome granite building forming a Town Hall, County Court and Market House has recently been erected on the side of the old market house. There is a large Union or Workhouse here and several large stores and handsome residences. Pa bought a couple books of views of Cornwall and Devonshire.

About half past one we started to Polperro. We had a delightful ride of eleven miles through a beautiful part of the country and arrived in Polperro about four o'clock. I think this place has a singular romantic situation. It is a little fishing port and is completely surrounded with very high hills. I said it was <u>completely</u> surrounded. I do not <u>quite</u> mean that for on one side of it there is the grand old ocean. Polperro is situated right in a hollow and contains about one thousand persons.[8] Some say that it was first inhabited by smugglers.[9] Mrs. Congdon met us at the gate with a very hearty welcome. She is a good motherly looking person and I think that I shall like her. They have two sons beside the one in Rockford, and four daughters. One of them is married and has a dear little girl called Jennie.

This afternoon it rained very hard. In the evening Mrs. Congdon went with us to Mr. Thomas Johns.[10] He looked very much like William and I should almost think it was him if I did not know better. His wife [Elizabeth] is rather tall and slim, has black hair and is very pleasant looking. They have one daughter [Mary Johns], a little girl of eleven years. She is a very delicate little thing and has been in the hospital in Plymouth for five months. They helped her a great deal but she is

8. Polperro is a 13th century fishing village, originally belonging to the ancient Raphael manor mentioned in the Domesday Book. Fishing has been the principal occupation of its inhabitants for centuries.
9. High taxes on goods imposed to finance the wars with America and France at the end of 18th century encouraged the Polperro fishermen to supplement their meagre livelihood by engaging in 'the trade' as smuggling was known.
10. Thomas Johns, brother of William (married to Lucy's sister Ann), who had remained in Polperro after the rest of the family had emigrated.

not well at all yet. From here we went to Mr. Giles'.[11] I think he is a very intelligent person and I like to hear him talk. I think he must have studied and read a great many books. Mrs. Giles is also a very pleasant looking person and I think I shall like her too. They have four sons. The eldest one has jet black curly hair and I think he is real pretty. There are three daughters beside the one in Rockford [Emma Congdon]. One of them is married [Mrs. Littleton] and lives in Plymouth, but is now on a visit here to her mother with her little boy. He is a dear little fellow, not quite two years old. His name is Frankie Hicks. I remained here all night but Pa and Ma went down to Mr. [Thomas] Johns.

11. John Giles, a family friend of the Rodds, living on Talland Hill, Polperro.

Polperro

Polperro, Cornwall, Wednesday July 6th, 1870

This morning Pa and Ma came up here to Mr. Giles and he went with us for a long walk. We went up to the top of a very high hill called the Wearring.[1] It is overlooking the sea, and the scenery was just grand. When we got near to the top we sat down under some rocks called Pleasure House. Then we went over near Talland bay and saw the church. They are both very interesting objects. In the church there are some curious relics of ancient feudal times. We walked back through the fields and down the old road to Polperro again. The streets are very narrow and irregular. Some say that Polperro was built one Saturday night when every one was in a dreadful hurry so as to finish up before Sunday, for the houses are built any-way and any-where.

On top of this high hill that we went up, there was once a very large house and beautiful gardens belonging to a rich gentleman. The Pleasure House[2] belonged to him also. But the house and gardens are all demolished

1. Probably The Warren which extends along the east side of the harbour in Polperro.
2. The 'Pleasure House' is believed to have been built at Lazy Cove, between Polperro and Talland Bay, by Captain Charles Kendall in the 18th century. It was still existing in 1802, when a fisherman named Zebedee Minards was granted a plot in the Warren to build a house for drying fish and fishing equipment, '20 feet long, commencing at the end of 220 fathoms . . . from a certain building called the Pleasure House otherwise Lazy Cove, towards Polperro'.

now. After dinner Mrs. Giles asked me up in the garden. We were obliged to go up a flight of stairs higher then the second story of the house to go to it. They have a nice collection of flowers and it was just lovely up there. The summer-house was so cool and nice. They also have a great variety of fruit and they were very fine. I ate an apple from Emma Congdon's tree. We went up to the end of the gardens in one of the summer houses and sat down and had a pleasant talk. She asked me all about how her daughter Emma gets along. The view from the garden was just splendid for it is up on a very high hill so we could see all around us.

About three o'clock I went down to Mrs. Johns and Mary played on the concertina for me. She plays very nicely. I remained there to tea then Lottie Giles[4] came after me to go for a walk with her. We went up to the top of Chapel Hill and climbed all over Chapel rocks and just had a delightful time. On the hill there was once a chapel owned by the Catholics. The tide was coming in and we watched the water dashing up against the rocks for a long time. Then we went up on Kayne, a hill eight hundred feet above the level of the sea. We sat down up there and ate apples and watched the people moving about in Polperro. They were so far below us, that they looked like little dwarfs. Then we went down by the sea again and watched the water in the moonlight. I thought it was just grand.

Polperro, Thursday July 7th, 1870

Today it was very pleasant, the sun shone out so bright and warm. This morning Ma wrote a letter home to brother William [Johns]. In the afternoon Pa and Ma came up to Mrs. Giles and we all went up in the

3. Charlotte Giles, born 1855, daughter of John & Emma Giles, family friends of the Rodds.

summer-house in the corner of the garden and we spent a couple of hours very pleasantly up there. Pa and Ma remained here to tea and then Mr. and Mrs. Giles and Lottie and Pa, Ma and myself went down on the rocks by the sea. We remained down there about two hours and I enjoyed myself very much indeed. I think Lottie is a very pleasant companion. She is so lively. She is six months younger then myself, but is much taller.

Polperro, Friday July 8th, 1870

About ten o'clock I went down to Mrs. Johns and found them all quite well. This morning we received two letters. One was from Evanston and the other was from home. They were all quite well. Sister Fannie said that they went to our Sunday School picnic and had a nice time. It was up the Rock river to the Rosendale Water Cure grounds. They were permitted to go into the house and take a drink of mineral water. Fannie said that Jennie Lake had received my letter and would answer it soon. Pa, Ma, and myself went up to Mr. Congdon to dinner. We had sago pudding.[4] I never tasted any before but I like it very much. After dinner we went over in their garden. It was a real nice cool shady little place. Mr. Congdon is a blacksmith and we went in his shop and I blew the fire with the large bellows. They were very large ones and it was real fun to use them.

In the afternoon Mr. and Mrs. Congdon and Pa, Ma, and myself had a nice long walk. We went up Landaviddy hill and saw Saint's Well. Then we went up Raphiel hill then back to Landaviddy. Then up Adams hill and Hardhead hill. The scenery from these high hills was grand. Sometimes our path was right along close to the sea then again we would be several hundred feet above

4. Sago pudding, made from the pith of a sago palm, was once a popular dessert in England.

the sea. Sometimes we would be walking over very rocky cliffs and sometimes down over green hillsides. On some of these high hills near the sea, there were little potato fields and Mr. Congdon said that the men that hoed the potatoes were obliged to tie themselves to an iron bar driven into the ground to prevent themselves from falling out over the rocks into the sea.

We went up Chapel Hill and down over Little Laney then back to Mr. Congdon's. Our walk was a very pleasant one and I enjoyed myself exceedingly. After tea Mr. and Mrs. Congdon and Pa, Ma, and myself went up to Mrs. [Priscilla] Littleton's, their daughter. They have a nice large house and a pretty place. After I returned to Mrs. Giles', Lottie and myself had a delightful moonlight walk down by the sea.

Polperro, Saturday July 9th, 1870

Today it rained very hard. I have not seen it rain so hard since I left home. Just before dinner I went to Mrs. Johns and Ma was writing letters. She wrote five letters, one to Evanston, one to Instow, one to Launceston, one to Buckland and one to Halifax. After dinner Lottie and myself took little Frankie Hicks and went up in the garden in the summer-house and remained there all the afternoon. Frankie is Lottie's nephew. He is nearly two years old and is just as cute as can be and can say almost everything. He is a real bright little fellow with light curly hair and blue eyes. He says "kangaroo" and "Garrisbaldi" and several other long words real plain. He called strawberries "stowbollies". When he had been a naughty boy he would say, "Naughty boy, naughty rogue".

In the evening there was a very large bonfire down on the beach. They always have one here the Saturday night before the Fair. It used to be a religious ceremony and the first one that jumped over the fire was cleansed from all their sins. They do not believe in this superstition now but still retain the custom of jumping over the fire. Lottie and myself went down and watched them a long while and sometimes the boys would nearly fall in the fire. Some of them got so warm while jumping that they would run to the river and dip their head and hands in the water and then go back to their jumping again.

Polperro, Sunday July 10th , 1870

This morning Mrs. Giles, Lottie, Pa, Ma, and myself went to chapel. It was only a few steps from their house. The text was from Solomon (5th chapter, part of the last verse). Pa and Ma remained to Mrs. Giles to dinner and tea. In the afternoon Pa, Ma, Lottie, and myself went to the Crumplehorn Sunday School anniversary. Crumplehorn[5] is a quarter of a mile from Polperro. The chapel was just crowded and a great many could not get in. Mr. and Mrs. Johns and Mary went. Mary rode there on a donkey. Mr. Congdon and family were also there.

A minister preached a short sermon from the text found in Ephesians (3rd chapter, 8th verse). The singing was splendid for they all sang with such a good will. Richard Congdon played the instrument and he seemed to understand music thoroughly. His sister and cousin sang a solo while himself and another cousin joined in the chorus. They sang it splendidly. All of the exercises were very good. I have the words of all the pieces that were sung and they are very pretty. After meeting Lottie and myself had a delightful walk up the Wearring. It was just splendid up there, it was so cool.

5. Crumplehorn was once a hamlet but is now part of Polperro. The watermill was formerly known as Killigarth Mill, mentioned in the Domesday Book.

In the evening we remained with Frankie and the rest went to Crumplehorn Chapel.

Polperro, Monday July 11th, 1870

This morning I went to Mrs. Johns and remained there to dinner. Ma did not feel very well today, it is the first time she felt poorly since we arrived in England. In the afternoon Mr. Congdon went with Pa, Ma, and myself to Mr. [William] Hocken's and took tea with him. He has a nice house and beautiful gardens. He is a very intelligent gentleman and it is very interesting as well as instructive to hear him talk. We had crab for tea but I never want to taste any again as long as I live, for it just about made me sick and Pa too, but Ma did not take any and I wish that I had not either but as I did eat some I was obliged to suffer the consequences.

After tea we all went out in the garden and ate some nice ripe gooseberries. The scenery from this garden was just lovely. We could see all of the Chapel rocks and Kayne. About eight o'clock Mr. Congdon took Pa, Ma, and myself to Looe.[6] It is a very pretty little place about three miles from Polperro. It is situated near the sea and has a very pretty beach. The harbor of Looe admits vessels of considerable tonnage and is protected from the fury of the Atlantic waves by a strong breastwork at the mouth of the river. Looe is quite a business place and a considerable amount of shipping etc. is done there. The band played through the streets of East Looe just before we left there and it reminded me of the band at home.

On our way back, Pa was taken sick. He felt so faint and weak he could hardly sit up but after a while he felt

6. Looe was originally two separate towns, East Looe and West Looe, joined by an estuary bridge in 1411. The twin towns had two Parliamentary seats, but lost them with parliamentary reform in 1832..

a little better so we drove on slowly. We got back to Mrs. Johns about eleven o'clock and as it was getting very late I went right down to Mrs. Giles'.

Polperro, Tuesday July 12th, 1870

This morning directly after breakfast I went to Mrs. Johns and found Pa but little better. Mrs. Hicks and little Frankie went away in the van. Until dinner time I amused myself by reading from a book entitled *John Ploughman's Talk* written by C. H. Spurgeon.[7] In it there is a very interesting and amusing chapter about monuments and gives a few funny inscriptions that I wish to write here:

Gentle reader gentle reader,
Look on the spot where I do lie,
I was always a very good feeder,
But now the worms do feed on I

Another: *Here lies the man who did no good*
And if he'd lived he never would
Where he's gone and how he fares
Nobody knows and nobody cares

Another: *Here lies returned to clay*
Miss Arabella Young
Who on the first of May
Began to hold her tongue

Another: *Here lies the body of Martha Gweyn*
Who was so very pure within,
She cracked the outer shell of sin
And hatched herself a cherubim.

Another: *Here lies the wife of Roger Martin*
She was a good wife to Roger – that's sartin.

7. Charles Haddon Spurgeon was a well-known preacher for most of the second half of the nineteenth century.

Another: *The Lord saw good - I was topping wood*
And down fell from the tree
I met with a check and I broke my blessed neck
And so death topped off me.

Here is one spelled as it was in the book:
Too Sweetur babes you nare did see
Than God amity gave to wee
But they were or taken with agur fits
And hear they ly's as dead as nits.

After dinner Lottie and myself took a nice story book and went up the Warren and sat down in a cool shady spot and had a nice time reading. Then we had a donkey ride over to Talland and saw the church. But we did not have a very good ride for the donkey was just as obstinate as possible. It would not go one bit faster than a walk but it would not go at all going uphill unless one of us went before it and pulled it along and the other went behind it and whipped it along so you see we did not get along with the animal very well. I suppose the trouble was that in the first place we were too kind and gentle to the poor creature.

After we returned to Polperro we went to the Fair but did not stay long for it commenced to rain a little. The fair commenced yesterday morning and lasts until Friday. This afternoon Mr. and Mrs. Johns and Mary and Pa and Ma went to the Crumplehorn tea meeting. Then they had a nice long ride. They went up Bullers hill and saw Kellow Farm or brother William's [Johns] birthplace. Then they went to Treweers and Longcross and saw Duckspool. Then they went to Mable Barrow and Windsor Green and Langreek then back to Polperro.

Polperro Wednesday July 13th, 1870

Today Pa, Ma and myself went down to Mrs. Congdon's to dinner. After dinner we went back to Mrs. Johns and Ma and myself both wrote a letter home. I told Fannie about our famous donkey ride and I know she will smile. In her last letter to us she said, 'Go to Rome, do as the Romans do' and now I think I have done so. Then Pa, Ma and myself went up to Mr. Giles to tea. After tea Ellen, Lottie and myself went riding. We went up Kellow hill and around that way to Pelynt. It is a little village about three miles from Polperro. We passed through the village and saw the church then we went back to Polperro around by the new road. We met Richard Congdon and sister and cousins riding. We had a very pleasant ride and I enjoyed it exceedingly. In the evening Lottie and myself went to the Fair a little while and were both treated to some candy and nuts.

Polperro Thursday July 14th, 1870

Today the sun shone out so bright and it was real warm. I went down to Mrs. Johns to dinner after which Mr. and Mrs. Johns and Mary and Pa, Ma and myself went to see Mrs. Hockens. We went up the new road and up around by Trelawny. Near here there are traces of an embanked and entrenched line of defense which is known by the name of Giants Hedge.[8] It is probable that it was a defensive earth work thrown up by the Danes.

Trelawny house was the residence of Sir John Trelawny and family, but they are all in London now. Only the gardener and wife were there to take care of the house and gardens. The house is a grand old mansion and has passed down through several generations. The

8. The Giant's Hedge is a large earth mound extending some seven miles across country from Looe to Lerryn. Its origin is unknown, and it may simply be a natural feature.

oil paintings were beautiful and are very old. Some of them were painted in the year 1500. Most of them were pictures of the Trelawny family.[9] The gardener's wife went with us through the principal rooms. We went in the drawing room, dining room, billiard room, library, study, Sir John's bedroom, his lady's bedroom, the spare bedrooms and dressing rooms. They were all furnished with very ancient furniture. There were several large halls and in the lower hall there were fourteen bells belonging to the different rooms.

Then we drove to Mrs. Bryant's (Mrs. Richard Johns' sister). We also saw her sister Mary and brother William, also their mother Mrs. Hocken. They all seemed very glad to see us and we spent a very pleasant afternoon there. Mrs. Bryant has three children all with curly hair. We remained there to tea and we had a cherry pie, also a junket. Then we had a drink of cocoa but I did not like it very well. It almost made me bad as the English call sick. Soon after tea we went back to Polperro for Mary Johns could not stand the night air. Our ride back was so very pleasant and I enjoyed myself exceedingly as also did Pa and Ma.

Polperro, Friday July 15th, 1870

Today it was very warm and dry. I went down to Mrs. Johns to dinner after which Lottie and myself went

9. The Trelawny family has a long history in England. In 1597 Sir Jonathan Trelawny was knighted by Queen Elizabeth I. His grandson, also Sir Jonathan, was the celebrated Bishop Trelawny who, along with six other bishops, was committed by King James II to the Tower of London for expressing in a petition his unwillingness to support the King. The prompt acquittal of the bishops prevented the people of Cornwall from rising in arms and led to 'The Song of the Western Men' as sung today:

And shall Trelawny live?
Or shall Trelawny die?
Here's twenty thousand Cornishmen
Shall know the reason why.

down on the beach over near Talland Bay and bathed our feet in the salt water. We had a delightful time but could not stay as long as we would have liked for the tide was coming in fast. Today we received two letters from America. One was from sister Fannie and the other was from Jennie Lake.

After tea Mrs. Giles went with Pa, Ma and myself to see some preserved fish which a man has collected from different bodies of water. Some of them he caught in Talland Bay and some in the Bay of Biscay. He is away now, dragging some part of the ocean and collecting specimens and curiosities for a gentleman. He has also given some specimen to the Queen's children. The fish were worth seeing and I am very glad I have had an opportunity of seeing them. One was the skeleton of one an angler caught in Talland bay with a sea gull in its mouth; the skeleton of the gull was in its mouth now. After we came back with Mrs. Johns, Pa, Ma and myself went up Landaviddy hill to Mrs. Hocken's. There is going to be a bazaar in Polperro next week and Mrs. Hocken has the things until then so we went up to see the things for we shall not be going to the bazaar. There was quite a number of articles and Ma and Mrs. Johns bought a few.

Our walk there and back was very pleasant and I enjoyed myself very much. Then Lottie and myself went down on the rocks for an hour and had a nice time. We counted over sixty fishing boats and sailing vessels out on the water. A great many fish are caught near here and the fishing trade is of considerable importance and I have heard that the dried whiting called 'buckhorn' prepared here is of excellent quality. Here is a verse about this fish that I have seen in a book:

"To eat buckhorn and drink tea
along with we,
May it please your Majesty
King William"

Polperro, Saturday July 16th, 1870

Last night I remained with Mary Johns. This morning we bid adieu to romantic little Polperro and the kind friends we have found there. First we went to Mrs. Giles and said goodbye to our friends there then we went to Mrs. Johns and said goodbye there then we went up to Mrs. Congdons. Mr. Giles and Mr. Congdon both gave us a few specimens from the mines near here. Then Mr. and Mrs. Congdon went with us to Tywardreath. We passed through Crumplehorn then on to Windsor Green and Mable Barrow where Doctor Couch of Polperro was buried.[10]

Then to Duckspool and Longcross and from there on to Polruan where we crossed over Fowey River on the ferry-boat to Fowey.[11] This town is romantically situated along the western bank of the river and close to its mouth. It is situated on a hill overlooking the harbor and is environed by woody heights. It was once an energetic seaport and in the time of Edward the Third it contributed forty seven ships and seven hundred and seventy men to his Calais-Bound fleet. The harbor is fine and capacious and encircled with the most lovely scenery. Vessels of a thousand tons can enter it at low water with perfect safety. In Henry the Eighth's time,

10. Dr. Jonathan Couch was a distinguished physician and naturalist, born in Polperro in 1789. After completing his medical studies he returned to Polperro in 1810 where he remained for rest of his life as the local physician, ichthyologist, and the author or many books including his *History of Polperro*, published shortly after his death in 1870.

11. Fowey is a Cornish port and centre of the Cornish china clay industry. The town is built upon the steep west bank of the Fowey estuary. Polruan, an ancient fishing village, lies on the opposite side of the estuary

the entrance of the harbor was guarded by forts on each side of the river with a chain extending across the harbor from the forts. A few links of this chain were dredged up by a fisherman some years ago. The town itself consists of one long irregular street, lying along the harbor at the extremity of which is the rope-walk, forming a convenient promenade, and commanding fine views of the river and surrounding hills and country.

Of late years, the most interesting event connected with Fowey is that of the royal visit in September. Her Majesty and Prince Albert arrived at the harbor from Falmouth and landed at the Victoria steps where there has been a fine large monument erected in memory of the occasion. At the end of the rope walk is situated the beautiful residence of Squire Rashleigh. The house is a splendid piece of workmanship and the gardens are lovely. They are called Point Neptune. The gentleman that owns the place is an invalid and way up on the cliffs from the house he has had the family vault built.[12] We went up and saw it and the work is very fine. The scenery from this point was magnificent. Then we went back past the house again. The marble mantelpieces in this house were cut by Mr. Congdon's son in-law. Going down the rope walk we passed several large houses and beautiful gardens and I enjoyed our walk very much. Then we visited the parish church. It is situated on the side of a hill to the west end of the town and was dedicated to St. Fimbarrus. Within the church we saw several monuments to the Treffry and Rashleigh families. While we were in the church a gentleman played on the organ for us.

12. The Rashleigh family were prominent landowners in and around Fowey for several generations. William Rashleigh built the mausoleum near his home at Point Neptune shortly before his death in 1871.

Then we visited Place or Treffry House,[13] the residence of one of the most energetic men of the day and contained a history in itself. The mansion is an embattled and brightly decorated structure and derives its name of 'Place' from palace. Within are many objects of curious interest and some splendid paintings. The dining-room is enriched with a carved ceiling of the time of Henry the Sixth and embellished with the coat of arms of Queen Elizabeth and others. The tower was constructed of white granite, one hundred and five feet in height. The gardens are beautiful and a walk of two miles can be made through them. It is all surrounded by a very high stonewall, just as the Castle gardens are in Launceston, and nature and art, magnificence and enterprise all combine to form a picture not soon to be forgotten.

From Fowey we rode on through Lostwithiel and Par to Tywardreath. Lostwithiel is pleasantly situated in a low valley on the western bank of the river Fowey, about six miles from its junction with the sea. There is a curious traditional account of Lostwithiel and it is this – 'That the town was once a city of considerable size but was swallowed up by an earthquake and that its present name is derived from that event: <u>Lost - With - All</u>'. Lostwithiel is evidently a town of great antiquity and appears to have been formerly the metropolis of the county. The church is built in the style of the fourteenth century. In the year 1644 it was used as a stable and the font formed a convenient watering trough. We arrived in Tywardreath about two o'clock. We had dinner to Mr. Odger's and spent a couple of hours there then we went to Par station where we bid farewell to Mr. and

13. Place Manor has been the home of the Treffry family since the 15th century. The house and gardens stand above the port of Fowey, with the town sheltering beneath the towers of Place.

Mrs. Congdon and took the train for Liskeard where we arrived about half past six.

At one of the hotels, Pa hired a conveyance and a driver to take us to Mrs. Hocken's, near Duloe. While we were in Tywardreath we went in a gentleman's garden. It was a lovely place and there was a great abundance and variety of fruit there. Down at the bottom of the garden there was a nice fish pond with nine or ten beautiful gold fish in it also three or four cute little sailing ships all fitted up nicely and sailing about, and there was a nice summer-house near where we sat down and watched the little fish and ships.

In Polruan opposite Fowey we saw the blacksmith's shop where Thomas Congdon used to work before he went to America. We arrived at Mrs. Hocken's about eight o'clock and she was very much surprised to see us. She was not very well, but her daughter Emma [Hocken] was quite well. I think that Emma looks more like Mrs. Richard Johns then either of the other sisters. Mrs. Hocken is such a pleasant motherly looking lady and I liked her as soon as I saw her. The scenery from her house was just splendid. We could see for miles on each side of us.

Devonshire

Tredinnick, near Liskeard Sunday July 17th, 1870

This morning Pa, Ma and Miss Hocken went to chapel and I wrote a long letter to Jennie Lake. In the afternoon it rained very hard, also in the evening so we did not go to chapel.

Tredinnick Monday July 18th, 1870

This morning I finished my letter and Ma also wrote a letter to sister Fannie.[1] This afternoon Mrs. Hocken, Pa, Ma and myself went over to Mr. William Hocken's and spent a very pleasant afternoon there. He is a very lively person and tried to make the afternoon as pleasant as possible for us and I did enjoy myself very much. His wife is a very quiet person but is also very pleasant. They have five children and they are all very healthy looking. Mr. Hocken had a harmonium and I played on it and sang every piece I could think of. He thought the two pieces entitled *Maggie* and *Jamie* were very pretty and I sang them over twice for him. Then he played and sang a piece entitled *The Vital Spark*; it was very pretty. Their house was a nice large one and the garden was lovely. It was so nice and cool there. We remained at Mr. Hocken's to tea then went back to his mother's, having spent an exceedingly pleasant afternoon with him.

1. This letter, now in the possession of Lucy's family's descendants, is reproduced in part opposite.

Tredinnick July 18, 1870
Dear ones at home

I must write to you today for tomorrow and Wednesday we expect to be traveling... we are indeed travelers and wayfarers for as soon as we get acquainted we have to gather up and go pitch our tent a little further on. We have met dear friends, yes everywhere they have done everything that could be done to make it comfortable for us, we met many dear friends at the so romantic old place Polperro and enjoyed their company and friendship very much, also the grand old scenery. We delighted to climb the old rocks and hills and gaze on the grand old ocean dotted over with vessels and fishing boats, but all things must come to have an end, so Saturday we had to bid adieu to that grand old place forever and all the kind friends there, it was pleasant to meet but sad to part. Many, very many were the tears shed but part we must, and we had no desire to have it otherwise for though it very pleasant to visit such a romantic old place and we became very much attached to the dear friends there, but we had no desire to make it our home, oh no far from that, indeed we have felt the least desire to take our abode in the most beautiful situation, but our mind wanders back to our western home and we feel a wish that our wanderings were over, thankful indeed shall we be if we are permitted to return to that dear spot and find all well...Lucy sends love to all and saith she is almost tired of traveling and shall be glad to get home although she has sure seen many interesting places and things and has enjoyed them finely. She and myself are very well we are thankful to say though I was poorly for a day or two but Pa is not nor was for several days. I think Polperro did not agree with him very well, it smelt so fishy and the steep hills to go up almost used him up and kept him so nervous, but we are away from that place and I hope he will soon feel well again then he will enjoy his visit again. We shall soon bid a lasting farewell to all this part of the country and hope to be in Instow in three days time, and get our roving done up. Then take a flying visit to Halifax, then back to Liverpool and home if the Good Lord will take care of us and we can trust him for his mercies never fail...

Remember us kindly to Wm. and Annie and both Mr. and Mrs. Johns and tell them their family remembers them. Much love from Pa, Me and Lucy

Tredinnick, Tuesday July 19th, 1870

This morning we bid adieu to the kind friends here and Mr. Hocken took us to Liskeard to take the half past nine o'clock train for Plymouth. While waiting in the depot we saw Mr. John Odgers, a brother to the one in Rockford. I think they look very much alike. Well, at last the train started and we were bound for Plymouth where we arrived about half past ten o'clock. We went to King Street where Mr. Odgers' sister, Mrs. Lang, lives and she was very glad to see us and to hear about her brother. I think they look a little alike. While we were at her house brother William's sister Elizabeth [Fiddick] and her little girl and baby [Emma and Bertha] came to see us. She looks most like her sister Mary [Elwick].

After dinner Mr. and Mrs. Lang and Pa, Ma and myself went out for a long walk. Plymouth was formerly called South Town or Sutton, and one of the commercial harbors of Plymouth is still called Sutton Pool. Plymouth was originally a little fishing village. The present name was adopted in 1439 in the reign of Henry the Sixth. In the time of Edward the First, the port possessed three hundred and twenty five merchant ships. At present, it carries on a large coasting trade, and its commerce with foreign ports amounts to upwards of fifty thousand tons per annum.

It has also, of late years, become a considerable port of emigration, principally to Australia. The town, being ancient, is irregularly built with narrow and tortuous streets except where modern improvements meet the old hap-hazard style of construction. Abandoned during the war to press-gangs and prize-crews resorting thither for the disposal of seizures at sea and the lavish expenditure of their proceeds, it may be supposed that neither elegance nor comfort made old Plymouth their abode. Yet it boasts some fine architectural structures. Plymouth was noted for its early Protestant tendencies and in the civil wars of the seventeenth century it always held to the Parliamentary side.

In the census of 1851, Plymouth contained 52,221 inhabitants. The harbor is a very fine one and is capable of accommodating one thousand merchant vessels. The erection of the Breakwater has added immensely to the security of the haven as a naval station, a commercial sea-port and a harbor of refuge. The Sound, across which this stupendous work of art is made to stretch, is about three miles wide of its entrance from the English Channel. On the west are the beautifully wooded heights of Mount Edgcumbe in this county of Cornwall, and on the north and east are the rugged shores of Devonshire.

The frequency of storms from the south west, in which direction the Sound was completely open to the long swell of the Atlantic, suggested the creation of an artificial barrier to the entrance of its waves. Accordingly in the year 1811, the Government resolved upon the undertaking, principally with a view to the convenience of the navy, then performing services of the utmost importance in the war with France. The first stone was deposited on the twelfth of April in the year 1812, and the work went rapidly on by the deposition of the largest blocks of stone that could be economically conveyed to the spot. These were brought in vessels constructed for the purpose and, being disengaged from the decks, were allowed to assume their own places at the bottom of the sea. Nearly four millions of tons of limestone were thus deposited, and in addition more then two million and a half of cubic feet of granite have been used to form the surface and sea slopes.

The total cost has been about one million and a half pounds sterling. The central portion of the Breakwater is three thousand feet long, in a line facing the ocean. At both ends, arms, together 1,000 feet long run backwards toward the shore at a angle of one hundred and twenty degrees. Two entrances of ample depth are thus left for ships, the eastern one being 1,000 yards and the western 1,600 yards wide. At the end of the western arm there is placed a lighthouse, sixty eight feet high. It was built between the years 1841 and 1844 of Cornish granite and divided into five stories. The eastern termination is marked by a pyramidal beacon, seventeen feet high and surmounted by a pole with a huge copper globe at the top. The Hoe itself is a public promenade and has been greatly improved of late years by the formation of carriage drives, foot paths, and seats for loungers who daily resort for fresh air and recreation to these 'Lungs of Plymouth'.

We went down to the Hoe and remained there for some times. The annual regatta took place while we were down there and the Sound was covered with the yachts collected for competition and pleasure boats of all sizes, and the Hoe from its commanding eminence, was alive with excited watchers. The military band also contributed to the enjoyment of the occasion. Several of the hotels of Plymouth were very large. Two of them each occupied a whole block. Some of the stores also were very large. We went back to Mrs. Lang's to tea and then went out again and now I wish to write about the Citadel. It occupies the high ground at the east end of the Hoe and is an irregular fortification dating from the period of Charles the Second. But many years before his reign, perhaps a century, there were wooden erections, called platforms. In the year 1591 it began to take the form of a solid and permanent structure and during the

Parliamentary struggle in the reign of Charles the First, the fort successfully resisted the Royalist attacks. It is now a massive erection of limestone and granite and is capable of mounting one hundred and twenty guns. The cliffs descend rapidly towards the sea, and on the slope there is a lower fort constructed amid the rocks. On the land side there is excavated all round a deep ditch and covered way. The entrance is given by two gateways with draw-bridges and within are the usual garrison accommodation and magazine surrounding the esplanade, the center of which is dignified by a colossal bronze statue of George the Second, habited as a Roman warrior. Joining Plymouth is Devonport. From the year 1691 until the year 1824 it was known by the name of Plymouth Dock.

The census of Devonport in the year 1851 was 50,150. The Dockyard is one of the finest in the world and comprises an area of seventy acres. Nearly four thousand men are employed there whose wages annually amount to 200,000 pounds. The Military Hospital is situated on the north side of Stonehouse Creek—a piece of water by courtesy, but during part of the time the tide is out, an expanse of mud. The buildings consist of four blocks or clusters ranged in a line and connected by an arcade. The hospital was built in the end of the eighteenth century of gray marble. It furnishes accommodation for five hundred patients. Within the fortified enclosure of Devonport is the Gun Wharf. It covers five acres of ground appropriated to the guns belonging to ships of war not in commission. In the open spaces between the storehouses are long ranges of cannons and huge pyramids of cannon balls. In other places are the gun carriages, whilst the upper floors of the storehouses are devoted to the reception of muskets, bayonets, pistols, cutlasses etc. used by seamen.

Plymouth, Wednesday July 20th, 1870

This morning Mr. Lang went with us to see the new chapel across the street from where he lives. It was a splendid structure built of granite. About half past twelve, Mr. and Mrs. Lang went down to the depot with us where we took the train for Exeter. Near Plymouth we passed over the Royal Albert Bridge, Saltash.[2] This lofty viaduct conveys the Cornwall Railway across the Tamar. Its total length is nearly half a mile over which distance it conveys a single line of rails by nineteen spans. The two central leaps of roadway overhang the water 910 feet. They meet in the center on a pier, formed of four cast iron columns, and the great weight is sustained by two segments of a huge circle of wrought iron tubing forming arches rising into the air, high above the passing train. The great main pier, on which the bridge is chiefly independent, is 240 feet high from its foundation in the bed of the river, and the tubes are 170 feet from the surface of the water.

Saltash is a quaint old town on the Cornish side of the Tamar which above it spreads into a lake. Its crazy old houses rise above one another on the slope. A greater part of the inhabitants are women and they are very expert and powerful in the management of boats and at the regattas they frequently win the prizes offered. The scenery along this road was lovely. For over fifty miles we rode along by the grand old ocean and passing through pretty little towns and villages. I remember while we were passing through a pretty place called Dawlish, we saw a pleasure boat, just the shape of a beautiful white swan, out on an inlet of the ocean, and it did look beautiful, gliding so gracefully over the waters.

2. The Royal Albert Bridge, a railway bridge spanning the river Tamar between Plymouth and Saltash, was completed by Isambard Kingdom Brunel in 1859, regarded as a great engineering achievement in its day.

We arrived in Exeter about three o'clock and remained there until half past six. Through England at all of the large depots there are book stands and newspaper stands. At the depot here we bought the book entitled *John Ploughman's Talk* written by C.H. Spurgeon.

About half past eight we arrived at the little station of Instow where cousin Fannie met us. It did not take us long to reach the house and at the door we were welcomed back again by Uncle, Aunt and Mary Ann. Uncle said that I did not look as well as when I left here but I suppose it is because I am tired, for ever since we left here we have been on the go all the time. After supper Fannie gave us a letter from home. It came yesterday. We did not expect one yet but was very glad to receive one. It said that they were all well at home.

Instow, Thursday July 21st, 1870

This morning the sun shown out very bright and clear. Directly after dinner Pa, Ma, Thomas, Fannie, and myself went down to the pier and Pa hired a man to row us to the sand hills. The wind was blowing quite hard so the water was rather rough and it made the boat toss and roll a great deal. First it made me afraid but after I got used to it I enjoyed myself very much. Pa lost his hat overboard into the water and it got wet inside and out, with the salt water, but it did not hurt it any. Some people say that salt water spoils everything it touches but it was not so in this case any way. We landed on the sand hills and then walked over to Westward Ho!, where a Fair or flower and dog show was held. It was just inside of the Pebble Ridge on the burrows and it was a splendid place for that purpose.

There were a great many people there and the band from Plymouth played for three hours. They charged thirty pounds or about one hundred and fifty dollars in American money. The display of flowers was very fine, though there was not such a large variety of them as we have at the fairs in Rockford. There were a great many dogs there from the Newfoundland and house dog down to the snarling little puppy and lap dog, and such a howling and barking as they did set up, it was really horrible.

Then we saw several dear little ponies, too. There was also a fine display of fruit such as pears, peaches, cherries, apples, grapes, plums, gooseberries, raspberries, and red, white, and black currants. While we were there, we saw Uncle Withecombe and Aunt Fannie and Cousin Martha and husband and Lewis and his wife and Sarah [Withecombe]. Then we all went over on the pebbles and sat down and had supper. About six o'clock a heavy fog just like a fine rain came in from the sea and made everything very wet so we went home. We walked back across the burrows and down through Appledore to the beach and were rowed across the river to Instow. The tide was out so the boat man could not row us clear up to the pier so we were obliged to walk over the wet sand and I can assure you that it was not very pleasant and we were very glad to get back to Aunt Sarah's again for we were very tired and hungry, and our feet were very wet. Thomas did not come home when we did but remained on the burrows nearly two hours after we left, but he did not get very wet, not near as wet as the rest of us did and we were obliged to change our clothes as soon as possible.

Instow, Friday July 22nd, 1870

Today it was very warm and sultry. There seemed to be scarcely a breath of wind stirring at all. This morning my feet were swollen so badly that I could not put on my shoes, I suppose it is because I was walking so much yesterday. I caught a terrible cold yesterday too and today I cough a great deal and am just about sick. I feel so dull and stupid I hardly know what to do with myself.

In the afternoon Ma, Mary Ann and myself went down on the beach. The tide was out and we walked nearly out to the river and I picked up a few pretty shells, but I did not enjoy myself very much for my head ached so badly, so we did not stay down there very long. In the evening the moon shone out very bright and clear, and it would have been just the night for a pleasant little walk if we had felt like having one.

Instow, Saturday July 23rd, 1870

Today also it is very warm and sultry, but not quite so much as yesterday, for the wind blows up quite cool once in a while. My cough seems to be worse today for I cannot even laugh a bit with out having a spell of coughing. In the evening Ma and Fannie went to Bideford to get a dressmaker to come here and help us a couple of weeks. They could not get one to come before a week from next Monday, although we would like one to come now.

While they were gone I amused myself by watching the trains pass, from the sitting room window upstairs. We did not take our walk on the beach this evening so I sewed a little and Fannie was working on a pair of slippers. I think they are for a present for Pa, I am not sure, but I know that they are very pretty anyway. She is working with purple, black, green, red and yellow zephyr.

Instow, Sunday July 24th, 1870

Today also it is very warm and sultry. The sun shines

out very hot. I did not go to chapel, but remained home with Fannie and Uncle. Aunt, Thomas, Mary Ann, Pa and Ma went. In the afternoon Fannie and myself went up to the chapel to hear an address delivered to the Sunday School and in the evening I heard the same person preach from the text found in Psalms (45th chapter, 15th verse). After preaching, Ma, Fannie and myself went up the Bideford road to meet Mary Ann [Rodd]. She went to Eastleigh that afternoon. We had a very pleasant walk and I enjoyed myself very much. The evening was so nice and cool, after the sultry day and the moon shone out so brightly too. We remained out walking until quite late.

Instow, Monday July 25th, 1870

This morning we did not go anywhere but in the afternoon Uncle, Aunt, Thomas, Mary Ann, and Fannie went into Bideford to have their pictures taken for us to take home. They had them taken together and they were first rate. I do not think that they could be better I went into Bideford with them and Auntie said she wished that I had my picture taken with them but we did not think of it soon enough so I could not. This afternoon Fannie and Mary Ann gave me a present of a beautiful gold locket, and I can assure you that I prize it very highly. I have wanted one for a long time and now I have got my wish. After tea it thundered and lightened a good deal but did not rain any. Fannie and myself went to the Post Office and we heard the Appledore church bells chiming and they sounded just splendid.

Instow, Tuesday July 26th, 1870

This morning we did not go anywhere for it so warm and sultry. My cough troubles me a good deal and Pa is so hoarse that he can hardly speak at all. Fannie too has a bad cough and in fact all of us that went to Westward

Ho! last Thursday are just about sick with colds. This afternoon Ma and Fannie went to Barnstaple, and while they were gone, Mary Ann and myself had a nice long stroll on the beach and sand hills and I enjoyed myself ever so much. Then we went to the station when the Barnstaple train came in and met Fannie and Ma. Today Uncle brought some nice ripe cherries home from Bideford and they were just splendid. After tea Fannie and myself had a nice long walk. The moon shone out very brightly and we remained out until quite late for it was so pleasant and cool after the hot and sultry day.

Instow, Wednesday July 27th, 1870

This morning I stayed up in my room and sewed and Fannie worked on a pair of slippers. In the afternoon the Sunday School had their tea meeting. They had it in one of Uncle's yards and Auntie baked all of the bread and cake for them. There was quite a number here besides the scholars and we had a first rate tea. After we had all finished eating, we went up on one of Uncle's high hills and had a splendid time. The children played the game of 'French Tag' and it was real interesting. We remained up there until after eight o'clock, then the children marched back to Uncle's, singing as they went. Then they stopped at Uncle's gate and gave three hearty cheers for Uncle and Aunt and then cheered their superintendent, after which they dispersed to the different homes. I think the pieces that they sang are very pretty and I have learned one entitled *The Reapers Song*.

Instow, Thursday July 28th, 1870

This morning Ma wrote a letter home to brother William. Just before noon Uncle took Pa, Ma, Auntie, Mary Ann and myself to Landkey to the mazard gardens. We passed through Fremington and Barnstaple and arrived in Landkey about two o'clock. We went to a friend of Auntie's named Mr. Dart. He has been married about six months and his wife is a very pleasant little lady and I liked her very much. They have a real pretty stone house and a nice yard. The scenery from there was just grand. We could see so many high hills and cozy little valleys all around us. We remained at Mrs. Darts an hour then they went with us to the mazard gardens. The mazards are like cherries only these are black and very sweet. The trees were very large ones and the leaves are very much larger and coarser than the cherry leaves at home. Some of the trees were just covered with mazards and they looked quite pretty. The mazards were nice large ones and Uncle bought several pounds. Ma is going to dry a few to take home so our friends can taste the English mazards. We remained at Mrs. Dart's to tea then went back to Instow. We stopped at Fremington to see Robert Withecombe's cousin, the one we saw at Buckland. We saw him and his wife also. She is a real pleasant person and their little boy is a smart black-eyed little fellow. Our ride home was very pleasant, and the scenery was grand. Of course we were obliged to go up and down several high hills for this part of England is very hilly indeed, but I have almost got used to the hills and dales now. We got back to Instow about half past eight o'clock, having spent an exceedingly pleasant afternoon and one which I shall long remember.

Instow, Friday July 29th, 1870

This morning Ma and myself prepared the mazards for drying and then put them out doors in the sun. Pa and Uncle went to Barnstaple market on the eleven o'clock train and came back in the afternoon on the four o'clock train. After tea Fannie and myself took a real pleasant little walk and I enjoyed myself very much indeed. There are not any frame houses in England at all, but the houses are all either stone or brick, though I believe I saw a few mud houses but I must confess, some of them could be more properly styled huts.

Some people here cannot imagine what kind of concern a frame building can be and are sure that we can not make everything as comfortable in one as in their stone and brick houses but I think they would find themselves mistaken.

Instow, Saturday July 30th, 1870

This morning Ma received a letter from Mr. Inman of Liverpool concerning the steamers of his line. He sent us a list of the steamers and the dates on which they sailed. The *City of Antwerp*, the one that we came in, sails August 13th but that is rather too soon for us. The *City of Paris* sails August 18th and I think likely we may go then. Today Ma wrote a letter Mrs. Eastcott, the lady that wishes to send her daughter part way with us. Ma wrote to her to tell her the day we expect to sail so if Annie Eastcott is going with us she will know when to meet us in Liverpool. After tea Mary Ann and myself took a short walk and then Thomas went with us. We had a very pleasant walk for the evening was so bright and clear but the night air did not agree with my cold very well for it made me cough a good deal.

Instow, Sunday July 31st, 1870

This morning Uncle bought us a letter from home and I can assure you that we were very glad indeed to receive it. They were all well but sister Fannie. She was not feeling very well and when Pa heard it, it almost made him homesick. I believe he would have started for home immediately if we had been ready to go. This morning Pa, Ma, Fannie and myself went to chapel. The text was from Philippians (3rd chapter, 10th verse). I did not like the minister very well for he acted as if he was only half awake. After dinner I took a book entitled *The History of a Nun* and went down by the water and spent a pleasant afternoon there reading. The book was a very interesting one. It told all about the sufferings and trials of a young lady while in a convent. She did not go of her own accord but was forced by her father to take the veil. I do not see how people can consent to go to a convent for life and be deprived of all worldly pleasures and shut themselves up from the company of dear friends and associates, I am sure I could not do it. This afternoon Mary Ann went to Sunday School and she wished me to go with her but I did not go for I was so much interested in my book. In the evening we all went to chapel but Uncle John. The text was from Matthew (25th chapter, 46th verse). The same minister preached this evening but you would not think it was the same one by his preaching for he spoke with such earnestness. I guess he slept a little while this afternoon for he was not one bit sleepy this evening. After we came home we went down by the water a little while and watched the tide coming in and I enjoyed myself very much indeed.

Instow, Monday August 1st, 1870

This morning, after breakfast I went down on the beach and remained down there a long time watching the tide coming in. We expected the dress-maker today but she did not come. She has been very sick and is not strong enough to sew yet. This afternoon Fannie went into Bideford on the four o'clock train and came back on the eight o'clock train. She tried to get another girl to come and sew for us but failed to find one. After tea Mary Ann and myself went down on the beach. The tide was coming in again and it was really amusing to watch it. We bathed our feet in the salt water but not long for I saw an ugly little crab creeping towards us and I expect if we had given it the chance, it would have given us the grip. It was real pleasant out in the evening and I enjoyed myself very much.

Instow, Tuesday August 2nd, 1870

Today it is very warm and sultry. There seems to be scarcely a breath of wind anywhere. This morning again I was down on the beach a little while. On the half past ten o-clock train, Uncle, Pa, Ma and myself went into Bideford. On the train we saw Mrs. Christopher Clement of Gillscott farm. She had been to Barnstaple to see the doctor for her husband. He is quite sick. He was not very well when we were at his house.[4] In Bideford we saw Christopher Clement's sister, Mrs. Heywood, also Abraham Clement and his wife. We went through the market and saw Aunt Fannie and cousin Martha and Charles and Robert and his wife. Then Ma, Auntie and myself went to see Ma's cousin. I think they look a good deal alike. She had a real pretty little gold-fish and some very pretty large and small shells. Her husband used to be a sailor and he got them in different countries. We went back to Instow on the half past four o'clock train. We found Fannie quite sick with a severe headache. She has never been very healthy. After tea Mary Ann and myself went out for a walk. The evening was bright and clear and I enjoyed myself very much.

Instow, Wednesday August 3rd, 1870

This morning Uncle brought us a long letter from home. They were all well as usual and Frankie still keeps inquiring when Pa, Ma and Lute will come home, and little Fannie May [Johns] wants to know if Aunt Lou is dead, for she can not see her any where.

4. Christopher Clement died in November 1870 at the age of 57.

Dear me, how I should like to see them all at home. Emma Johns has received my letter and I shall expect an answer in two weeks. Today Ma and myself were sewing nearly all the time. About three o'clock the dressmaker came and took some sewing home. This afternoon Fannie gave Pa a present of a beautiful pair of worked slippers, and he thinks a good deal of them for she worked them herself. In the evening Fannie, Pa, and myself went down on the beach and sat down by the water a long time.

Instow, Thursday August 4th, 1870

Today it rained a good deal so it was real wet and disagreeable out of doors. All the morning I was engaged in writing a good long letter to the dear ones at home. We write one home every week but this week Ma was so busy sewing that I wrote in her place. I covered two sheets and a half with my nonsense. After tea Fannie and myself walked in to Bideford. We got their pictures and they are splendid. Uncle never had his picture taken before and he would not have had it taken now, only we want one to take home with us. I bought a little book entitled *Language of Flowers*. It only cost six pence or about fifteen cents and I think that was very cheap, but I think that books are much cheaper in England than in America. We called on Mr. and Mrs. Rigsby, and I think that they are very pleasant people indeed. They keep a little store near the bridge and we go in there to rest a few minutes nearly every time that we go into Bideford. Fannie and myself went back to Instow on the eight o'clock train and then Ma went with us for a short walk. It had stopped raining and the evening was very pleasant and cool. We went up around by the Post Office and I posted my letter then down by the sea and had a nice walk along on the sand and I picked up a few shells. I enjoyed myself very much.

Instow, Friday August 5th, 1870

It was very warm and sultry all day. I have had another beautiful present given me. This morning Uncle and Auntie presented me with a beautiful gold chain and I can assure you that I prize it very highly indeed. I have long wanted a gold locket and chain and earrings and now I have realized my wish.

This afternoon Fannie and myself sat upstairs in my room a long time. I was sewing and she was crocheting on a tidy[5] for Ma. It is a very pretty one and is far superior to anything that I have ever seen before, worked with tidy-cotton. Today Mary Ann gave Ma two handsome lamp mats that she made herself, and Thomas gave me a beautiful large shell. I am going to take home to Frankie [Kyle] a 'Jumping Jack' that was bought at the Crystal Palace[6] London, at the first exhibition there. It is a real funny little 'Turk' and was bought for Thomas when he was a little boy, two or three years old. Now he is going to send it home to Frankie. After tea Pa, Ma, Mary Ann, Fannie and myself went down on the beach to the mussel rocks. The mussels were so thick that we could not walk without stepping on a good many. We saw a man down there raking up a cartfull to sell. Some people eat them, and cockles too, but I am sure that I could not eat either of them, nor limpets or winkles either. I think it would be even worse then eating crab and I am sure that would be needless. The cockles are found in the sand. When the tide is coming in, you may discover their hiding place by a very small hole in the sand, directly above the fish. Fannie and myself tried to dig a few but it was getting

5. A tidy is a decorative protective covering for the arms or headrest of a chair.

6. The Crystal Palace was a huge glass and iron structure originally built for the Great Exhibition of 1851. It was then moved and rebuilt in Sydenham in 1854. Queen Victoria performed both opening ceremonies. It was destroyed by fire on November 30, 1936.

too dark to see the holes. After we went home, Mary Ann and myself had a delightful moonlight walk on the Bideford road.

Instow, Saturday August 6th, 1870

Today Ma and myself are busy sewing again. This morning we received a letter from Aunt Fannie. They were all quite well and are coming into Bideford to see us for the last time next Wednesday. I answered the letter for Ma and sent it by the next mail. In the evening Ma, Fannie and myself went out for a little walk and I enjoyed myself exceedingly. After we got back it rained real hard and it did a great deal of good too for the ground was getting very dry and hard.

Instow, Sunday August 7th, 1870

This morning Pa, Ma, Uncle, Mary Ann, Fannie and myself went to chapel. Mr. Restarick, a gentleman we saw at Westward Ho! preached an excellent sermon. He came to Auntie's to dinner after which he and Fannie, Ma and myself went down to the beach and spent a couple of hours very pleasantly there. I think that Mr. Restarick is an exceedingly pleasant person and I like him very much indeed.

He lives in Bideford and owns a large Rope Manufactory on the other side of the river. We all went to chapel in the evening but Uncle John. Afterwards, Mary Ann, Fannie and myself walked half way to Bideford with Mr. Restarick. After we got back home it rained quite hard.

Instow, Monday August 8th, 1870

Today again Ma and myself are busy sewing so we did not go out anywhere until after tea. Then Uncle, Aunt, Pa, Ma, and myself went up on the hill and over in the orchard. I saw 'Tibby' but she is getting so very independent that she would not come near us at all. After we got back Mary Ann and myself went for a walk. We went up past the chapel then around by the sea and back around to the station. There we sat down on the settee on the platform a long time and had a cozy little chat together. The moon was shining very brightly and we remained out there until about half past ten and I can assure you that we both enjoyed ourselves very much indeed.

Instow, Tuesday August 9th, 1870

We remained in the house all day and were very busy sewing again. Fannie presented Ma with a beautiful crocheted tidy and Uncle and Auntie gave her a nice ink-stand. In the evening Fannie and myself went over to the Park but did not stay long for her ladyship, Mrs. Cleveland was out around surveying her premises and we did not care about facing her majesty. The woman that lives at the Lodge gave us some lent-lily roots.

Instow, Wednesday August 10th, 1870

This morning about seven o'clock Fannie and myself went up to the Park again. This time her ladyship was not up yet. We went up on the hill where the monument is and dug up a few snow-drops and white sundie roots. After we got back, Ma and myself partly packed our trunks for tomorrow we leave here and are going up to Yorkshire to see Mr. John Baume. About half past one o'clock, Thomas, Pa, Ma and myself went into Bideford. Uncle Withecombe and Aunt Fannie met us at the station. They had been waiting for us nearly two hours. A regatta between the Bideford and Barnstaple clubs took place on the river near Bideford today. The shore on both sides of the river and the bridge was thronged with excited watchers, and numerous pleasure-boat with anxious occupants were sailing slowly along near the shore. The Bideford club came out victorious, and won the prize.

Auntie gave me Cousin Ellen's picture. It is very much like her. I do not think that it could be more natural. We wanted Uncle's and Auntie's pictures too but did not get them. Uncle never has had his taken and says he is too old to have it done now. He said he would feel "as silly as a young man going courting" or 'sparking' as he calls it.

When we went back to Instow, they both went to the station with us and there we bid each other a very sorrowful farewell. We returned to Instow by the half past four o'clock train. After tea Mary Ann and myself went down on the beach together for the last time. It was very pleasant down there and we remained a long time watching the pleasure boats coming down the river from the regatta. We also saw the canoes. They were very long and narrow. This evening the tide was nearly out, and the water was very calm and still, but today when we were in Bideford the tide was coming in and it was dashing up against the pillars of the bridge and rushing and roaring through the arches at a great rate. I thought that it was really grand. While we were down on the beach, Miss Young came down and bid me good bye. Then Mary Ann and myself called on Mrs. Snow also on Miss Bready, the school-mistress. I think they are both very pleasant ladies. We also called on Miss Norman and I bid them all good bye. After we returned, we all had a glass of elderberry wine. It was very good but rather strong. Auntie made it more then ten years ago she said.

Instow, Thursday August 11th, 1870

This morning we arose about five o-clock and we got everything packed and ready by half past-six. We had no appetite for breakfast so Auntie put up a lunch for us. About half past seven we bid adieu to dear Auntie and Uncle, Mary Ann, Thomas and Fannie [Rodd] went over to the station with us. There we bid each other a sorrowful farewell, and were soon on the train bound for Halifax and leaving dear friends and pretty little Instow behind us. I was obliged to carry my doll in my arms for the trunks were both full. We passed through Exeter about ten o'clock and arrived in Bristol about one, where we remained until three. I should not like to live in either of those places for there was so much noise and bustle there. It made me think of Chicago. We passed through several very large places between Bristol and Halifax, namely – Gloucester, Birmingham, Worcester, Derby, Chesterfield, Sheffield, and Wakefield. We passed through the counties of Somerset, Gloucester, Worcester, Warwick, Derby, and part of Yorkshire. Most of the large cities that we passed through were manufacturing places, and in the night the fires from the foundries looked grand. In some places the towns looked as if they were all on fire.

We arrived in Halifax, Yorkshire, about eleven o'clock at night. There was no <u>bus</u> or <u>cab</u> at the depot and Mr. Baume was not there to meet us either so we did not know where to go. First Pa put our trunk in the cloak-room and then we went to see if we could find a hotel. Some places had not any room for us and at other places, they said that it was against their rules to take anyone in after midnight, so we had nowhere to lay our weary heads down to rest. Then we tried to find Mr. Baume's house, but think of trying to find anything in a town of over seventy thousand inhabitants, anyone might as well try to find a needle in straw-stack. Some times we would meet a straggler like ourselves and we would enquire of him where Mr. Baume lived – then we would see a light in some window and Pa would knock and enquire of them, but alas! no one knew where he lived, and some did not think there was anyone called by that name. And so we wandered on from house to house and from street to street until after two o'clock in the morning, when we had the good luck to meet a woman that knew just where Mr. Baume lived so she took us right to his house. Of course they were all in bed but we woke them up and he came to the door to let us in. He seemed very glad to see us and said if he had known that we were in town he would not have been able to sleep one bit until he had found us. He had not received our letter, stating what day we would be in Halifax. Mrs. Baume got up also to welcome us. She is a good motherly looking person and I think that I shall like her. She has a queer accent with her speech. I think she is Scotch. We did not talk much but retired to rest, for we were so very tired.

Thomas Johns (1830-1904), at whose home
in Polperro Lucy and her parents stayed in 1870

Polperro harbour, viewed from Talland Hill in 1870

Point Neptune, Fowey, Cornwall, visited by Lucy in July 1870

The Royal Albert Bridge between Plymouth and Saltash, photographed in 1864, five years after it was opened.

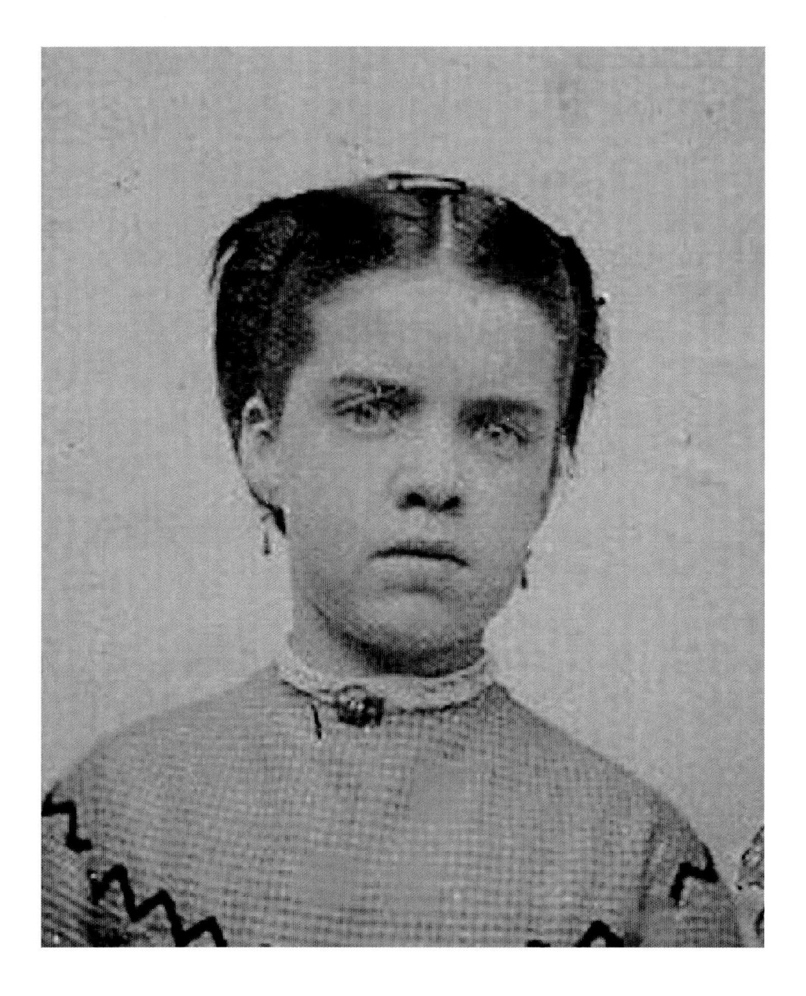

One of the few surviving portraits of Lucy,
probably taken shortly before her voyage to England

Lucy as a child (left, standing) with one of her young nieces and (right) at her home in Rockford, Illinois USA

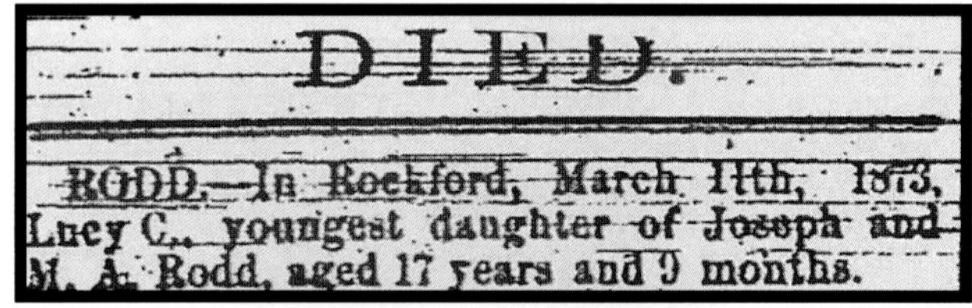

DIED.

RODD.—In Rockford, March 11th, 1873, Lucy C., youngest daughter of Joseph and M. A. Rodd, aged 17 years and 9 months.

Lucy's death notice in March 1873 and the stained glass window erected in her memory in Rockford

Yorkshire

Halifax, Yorkshire, Friday August 12th, 1870

This morning we did not get up very early, for we were dreadful tired and sleepy. Yesterday we were up twenty one hours out of the twenty four. Mr. [John] Baume has five sons and two daughters. The baby is a dear little girl five months old. The next older is a little girl called Nettie [Baume]. She is a little younger then Fannie May [Johns] and looks very much like her. The boys are five, nine, sixteen, eighteen, and twenty years old. They all have red hair like their father except the one sixteen years old. He has dark brown hair. Mr. and Mrs. William Baume came to see us. They are very pleasant people and I like them exceedingly. They have three children, one boy and two girls. The eldest is eleven years old.

This morning Ma wrote two letters. One was to Evanston, the other to home. In the afternoon about three o'clock Mr. Baume got a cab and took Mrs. W. Baume and daughter and Pa, Ma and myself out riding. We rode around for an hour and had a real pleasant time. We passed through the principal streets and saw a number of public buildings. The Court House is a very large building, made of white stone. The work on the exterior is very fine. We visited the church yard where Mr. J. Baume has two or three children buried. He has a brother buried there also. Near the churchyard we saw high rocks and cliffs. And they were just black with the smoke from the foundries. And the trees and fences were black too. There are two hundred foundry chimneys in Halifax.

Then we visited the [Crossley Porter] Orphanage. It was a magnificent building and the workmanship on the outside was very fine. The building cost 55,756 pounds. It was built and furnished by Mr. John Crossley Esq., Mr. Joseph Crossley Esq., also Sir Francis Crossley, Baronet and Member of Parliament. An annual endowment of 3,000 pounds is given for its support by the same gentlemen. There were two hundred and ten orphans in the building. Seventy five were girls and the remainder were boys. They take them as young as five years old and keep them until they attain the age of sixteen. The principal went with us through the rooms namely: the bed rooms, the dining room, kitchen, buttery, meat room, milk room, bake room, bath room, and play rooms also the laundry. They washed and ironed every day and the baker baked several hundred loaves of bread eight times a week or twice a day. Then we saw the sewing room where two or three ladies are engaged in sewing every day.

After leaving the Orphanage we visited the Park. It was donated to the public by Sir Francis Crossley. The citizens of Halifax have erected a statue, as large as life, of him, reclining in an arm-chair, in the park. Mr. Baume said it was a perfect picture of him. The park was a lovely place. There were several splendid statues there and pretty trees and a nice large fish-pond besides a great variety of beautiful and choise flowers and plants. We also saw the nice large almshouses[1] given to the poor by one of the Crossley brothers.

1. Living in the almshouses was conditional upon being at least 60 years old, without adequate means of support, of good character, having had a religious upbringing, and being incapacitated from work by age, disease or infirmity.

We got back to Mr. Baume's house about tea time, having enjoyed ourselves very much indeed. In the evening I went over to Mr. William Baume's and remained with Emily all night. They have a rather large house three stories high.

Halifax, Saturday August 13th, 1870

I remained with Emily to breakfast then went to Mrs. J. Baume's. Mr. Baume went with Pa and Ma and myself for a walk. We saw the buildings belonging to the Crossley carpet concern.[2] There are several buildings belonging to the establishment. One of the mills was ten stories and all of the others were eight stories. There are fourteen mills and five sheds, I think. They burn one hundred and twenty tons of coal a day and make more then 100,000 yards per week. Eight thousand workmen and eighty book keepers are employed to attend to the business and they receive thirty shillings of English money or about nine dollars of American money per week. Yesterday we went through the principal streets of Halifax but today we passed through a few of the old streets and I saw that there were beggarly and disgraceful characters in the town of Halifax, as well as the educated and refined class.

Then we visited a very old church. It formerly belonged to the Catholic denomination and was probably built in the eleventh century. There was a large sun-dial on the tower. The church yard was just covered with slate tombstones. In some places there were two or three layers of graves and so the yard is so full that they are not allowed to bury any more there. The church

2. John Crossley founded his carpet mill in Halifax in 1803. By 1900 it had become the largest carpet factory in the world, employing nearly 5000 people and leading to the expansion of Halifax, England from a small wool trading town into a prosperous industrial centre.

will seat about one thousand and the seats are all carved beautifully. I think they are oak and the doors too, which are also handsomely carved. The ceiling consisted of the 'coat of arms' of the rich and influential men of the church.

While we were there we had the privilege of seeing a dozen couples married and as we were leaving the church we met six couples more. One of the brides was nearly sixty and the bridegroom must have been over seventy. I guess neither of them were ever married before for they both acted so silly. As we walked behind them down the street I saw her look at her ring and then look up to her husband, smile so sweetly, then look at her precious ring again just as if she had never had one before. The husband did not seem to be quite so much pleased, but of course he answered back the sweet smile of his charming bride. It was quite laughable to watch them. The gentleman had a bundle under his arm. It was tied up in a red cotton pocket handkerchief. I presume it contained bread and cheese for their wedding dinner. In the afternoon Mr. Baume went with Pa, Ma and myself through the market. The building was a very large one and the display of fruit, vegetables, meat, and cheese was very good indeed.

Halifax, Sunday August 14th, 1870

This morning Mr. Baume and Pa went to chapel but Ma and myself remained home with Mrs. Baume. When they came back, Mr. Baume went with Pa, Ma and myself over to Mr. W. Baume's to dinner, and to spend the afternoon there. Emily has a very large harmonium and a piano. The harmonium had fourteen stops besides the knee-swell and was a very rich sounding instrument. Emily can play very nicely on it. She played and sang two very pretty pieces entitled *The Vital Spark* and *Shall*

We Know Each Other There. We spent an exceedingly pleasant afternoon with Mrs. W. Baume and daughter while the gentlemen went to chapel. Yesterday evening Mr. Baume's sister and husband called on us. I do not think that she looks very much like either of her brothers. She has black hair and eyes and is quite pretty I think. She is an exceedingly pleasant person and her husband is very pleasant too and I like them both very much. This evening Ma and myself went back to Mrs. J. Baume's and Pa went to chapel with Mr. Baume. After chapel Emily came over after me so I went over with her and remained all night.

Halifax, Monday August 15th, 1870

This morning Mr. Baume went with Pa, Ma and myself for a walk. First we visited All Souls Church.[2] It is an exceedingly handsome piece of workmanship, built in the year 1859 of white stone. But it is blackened up so with the smoke from the different foundries that anyone would suppose from looking at the church that it is several hundred years old. The interior of the church was beautiful. The pulpit and font consisted of different colored marble and the windows were colored glass. One window cost between three and four hundred pounds of English money or nearly two thousand dollars in American currency. The organ was a magnificent one having three thousand and sixty one pipes. Then we went one hundred and thirty steps to the bell-room. There were eight bells and the first peal was rung on February 23, 1861, consisting of 5,024 changes in one continued course or in three hours and twenty seven minutes. From the bell room to the top of the tower there were fifty steps more, making the whole number of steps from the bottom to the top of the tower one hundred and

2. All Souls Church was closed in 1978.

eighty and being the highest tower that we have had the privilege of going up. From here we went to see the opening of the new North Bridge.

The mayor made a speech then a procession consisting of several handsome carriages, containing the band and mayor and corporation of the town, drove over the new bridge. As soon as the procession had passed we walked over it, then went back to Mr. Baume's to dinner. In the afternoon we walked down town and enjoyed ourselves walking through some of the principal streets until tea time. In the evening Mr. and Mrs. Walton came to see us and we spent a couple of hours very pleasantly with them talking about America etc.

Halifax, Tuesday August 16th, 1870

This morning Ma and I did not go anywhere but Pa and Mr. John Baume went down to the agent for the Inman Line to see about the steamers. Mrs. J. Baume does all her work besides taking care of the baby and it is quite peevish now for it is teething. Well, I took care of the baby a little while for her this morning. It is a pretty little thing and very smart for a child only five months old. And Nettie is a dear little thing, she reminds me so very much of Fannie May in her actions and features though Nettie has fire red hair and in fact five of them out of the seven have hair like their father's.

In the afternoon we went down town and bought a few more things. Ma bought more velvet for a sack for sister Lizzie and she also bought a cloth sack for me. I like it very much and it is a good warm one for winter, but I am afraid it is not as they will wear in Rockford next winter. Then Pa and Mr. J. Baume went to see about the steamer, but the agent said it was full and we could not go. We did not know what in the world we would do for tonight Mrs. Eastcott and Annie (Eastcott)[3] will get into Liverpool waiting for us and if it was not for that we would not think of going until next Tuesday for then the *City of Antwerp* sails. She was appointed to sail last Saturday, but did not go, but if we had known it we would have not made any arrangements to go before. Well, then the agent telegraphed to Liverpool that we must go if possible and we had a telegram back that it was impossible, but Pa had paid the deposit money and they were bound to take us or pay our board until next Tuesday. So tomorrow morning by the first train, Pa and Mr. Baume is going to Liverpool to see about the boat and leave us here in Halifax until they send us a dispatch whether we will go or not.

Halifax, Wednesday August 17th, 1870

This morning Mr. Baume went with Pa on the seven o'clock train into Liverpool to see about the steamer. Ma and myself packed our trunks then Emily and myself went to the Post Office. I got three letters from America. One was from Evanston, and the others were from Rockford. The letter said that our friends were all quite well both places. About three o'clock we received a telegram from Pa telling us to meet him in Liverpool as soon as possible so we hurried and got ready and bid good bye to our friends in Halifax and Mr. W. Baume took us to the depot. I gave my doll to Nettie for there was not room for it in the trunk and I did not want to carry it in my arms. While we were waiting at the station a train went out the other way and just as it started out a very large fleshy woman with a big basket on the arm, rushed onto the platform to go onto the train

3. Annie Eastcott was from Launceston and was being sent to Minnesota to live with her aunt. Annie's mother asked that she travel with the Rodds as far as possible. Nothing more is known of what happened to her after her arrival in the USA. with Lucy.

and when she found that she must be left behind she set down her baskets, put her hands on her hips and pouted for at least five minutes. It was really quite laughable to watch her.

Soon our train came whistling into the depot so we said a hurried good bye to Mr. Baume and were soon off bound for the city of Liverpool. We passed through fifteen tunnels traveling the sixty miles. The scenery was very grand. One place looked almost like Polperro, Cornwall. We arrived in Liverpool about eight o'clock, passing through Manchester and several other places of importance. We saw Annie Eastcott and her cousin also his brother. Then we all went to the hotel where we had supper and spent the night there.

At Sea Again

Liverpool, Thursday August 18th, 1870

This morning we had breakfast at the hotel then went down to the depot and got our things, and then took a cab and went down to the pier. But I forgot to say first that in the morning Pa and Ma went to Mr. Jones. He was not at home, but Mrs. Jones was very glad to see them and they then went through the Rope Manufactory. While they were gone, Annie and I remained at the hotel and I amused myself by playing on the piano. Then we went down to the wharf where the tender was waiting to take us to the steamship *City of Paris*[1]. It is four hundred and sixty feet long, and forty feet wide, it burns from ninety to one hundred tons of coal in twenty four hours besides what is used for cooking purposes. The officers are very polite and gentlemanly. There are eighteen fireman, twelve engineers, and one boiler maker among the crew. The number of passengers is one thousand, the majority, of course, are steerage.

The wharf was thronged with eager watchers and soon we reached the steamer. The boat was all hurry and bustle, one running this way and one running that, some

1. The *City of Paris* was built for the Inman Line in 1865 for transatlantic voyages. Tonnage 2556, length 346 feet, one funnel, three masts, iron construction, single screw, and speed of 13 knots. She broke records for the passage to Halifax from Queenstown in August 1869. In May 1870 she had an extensive rebuild, her tonnage increased to 3500 and lengthened to 398 feet. In 1884 she was sold to French owners and in March the following year she collided with a French steamer in fog off Malaga and sank.

sick and some well, some packing and some unpacking and it was a state of confusion till the tender left us and then soon we were off, leaving Old England and the dear friends we found there, but sailing to America in hope of seeing still dearer friends and places and I wish I was home this very minute. Oh would not I jump for joy too, as Frankie (Kyle) says. When we had been on board an hour or two the steward handed us a letter and it proved to be from Instow from Cousin Fannie. They were all well and she said she wished she was here. This afternoon we have very strong head winds so cannot go very fast. Well I have had the privilege of feeling the pleasure of sea sickness, but I shall deem it a still greater pleasure if I am not sick any more and I hardly think I shall be. I have remained up as long as I can, but I think now I must turn in as they say. We have to sleep in the ladies' saloon so it is not quite so pleasant as it would be if we had a room alone, but we must put up with it for the cabins are full.

At Sea, Friday August 19th, 1870

This morning I feel first rate and do not feel one bit sick. We got to Queenstown and I plan on sending a letter to Instow to answer the one cousin Fannie sent me. We have not been out of sight of land yet and will not until tonight. We got in the harbor at Queenstown about noon today and the tender came to take all who would like to go ashore until the mail came. A good many went and a gentleman, Mr. Green of New London, Canada, got off there and he offered to take Annie and I. We went. Pa and Ma did not care to go at first, but after we came back they said they wished they had gone, but it was too late to wish then.

Well, in a few minutes we landed on Irish ground and we saw Patrick and Bridget at home sure enough and they talked Irish to perfection too, at least I think it for we could not understand one word hardly. And such a lot of beggars I never saw before, why a half dozen would follow us for a block or so and if you put your hand in your pocket once that would not be the last time by any means. Queenstown is not such a large place as I thought and the buildings are not anything extra either. There were a few nice large buildings and we walked around through several streets and then went to the refreshment rooms and had a glass of lemonade and a cake and an Irish apple and rested a little and then walked around again, but I did not enjoy it very much for the streets and people are so dirty. At half past three the tender left the pier so by three o'clock we found ourselves on board the *City of Paris* again.

About half past four the sailors weighed anchor and we were once more sailing towards beloved America and leaving dear friends behind us but hoping to see still dearer friends in our far-away home. After we had started the steward gave us a letter and it proved to be from Emma Johns. They were all well as usual and she said she expected a letter from me before, but better late then never. The last time I saw her was the day before we came away. I wonder if I shall see her the day after we get home. I feel first rate this evening. I do not believe I shall be sick any more, but sick or not I wish I was home and I hope to be there before two weeks longer. On Fastnet Rock, a few miles off the southern most point of Ireland is an iron light-house with a revolving light which gradually increases and decreases every two minutes. The rock rises about sixty feet above high water mark. This light-house was erected in the year 1848. It is a circular tower ninety two feet high. This light is visible for eighteen miles. I must close now for I must retire for it is getting quite rough.

At Sea, Saturday August 20th, 1870

Today the weather was very warm and bright. There was scarcely a breath of wind at all so the water was very calm and still. Of the two hundred cabin passengers, over one hundred are sea sick and you may picture the scene if you can for I cannot begin to describe it. The number of miles between Liverpool and Queenstown was about two hundred and forty five. Between Queenstown and Cape Clear or Fastnet Rock about sixty miles. From the time we left the rock to this day noon we have sailed one hundred and eighty nine miles.

At Sea, Sunday, August 21st, 1870

This morning it rained for a while quite hard then it cleared up and was real bright and warm. Pa, Ma and myself are not feeling very well and I remained up on deck in the open air nearly all day. This morning there was services in the dining saloon but only a few attended for so many are sea sick. From yesterday noon until today noon we sailed three hundred and twenty eight miles. This afternoon we saw hundreds of fish rolling around in the water. I think that they were what we call the porpoise.

At Sea, Monday August, 22nd, 1870

Today we have very favorable winds and we have gone faster then yesterday. Between yesterday and today noon we sailed three hundred and thirty miles. We all feel a little bit better today. In the afternoon we saw a great many dear little birds following the steamer. The sailors called them Mother Carey's chickens.[2] It seemed

2. In the 18th century, mariners called the petrel 'Mother Carey's Chicken', or 'Carey's chick' and believed its appearance to be an omen of bad weather. The origins of the name are unclear, but it has been suggested that in seamen's lore Mother Cary was the name given to a water spirit, whose 'chickens' were the souls of drowned sailors.

good to see the birds so far away from land. I do not know whether they were land birds or not. We have seen a great number of sea gulls also. I used to think that the ocean was just full of whales and sharks and that I should see hundreds and even thousands of them but I find that I was greatly mistaken for we only see a whale once in a while, off a long way from us.

At Sea, Tuesday August 23rd, 1870

This morning also we had very favorable winds and sailed since yesterday noon three hundred and twenty one miles. Today I feel very much better but do not dare to venture down to my meals just yet. In the afternoon a very rough wind blew up and in the evening the wind blew a perfect gale. The water was very rough and the ship tossed and rolled very much indeed. Several times the water came in over the lower deck and once or twice the water came in over the top deck. While we remained up on deck we were obliged to hold on to the railing to keep from falling and after I retired to my berth I was obliged to hold on to the sides with both hands to prevent myself from rolling out.

The trunks in the passage and rooms rolled from one side to the other and every time the steamer gave a sudden pitch the ladies would scream and cry for the stewardess to go to them, just as if she could keep the wind from blowing or the steamer from rocking so. It continued to be rough until three o'clock in the morning.

The captain said he was obliged to keep four men at the wheel to guide the steamer, while in calm weather only one man is required for that purpose. We were all very glad indeed to see the morning light and also thankful that we were brought through the night safely.

At Sea, Wednesday August 24th, 1870

This morning we have very strong head winds so we do not get along so fast. Since yesterday noon we have sailed two hundred and ninety six miles. Early this morning there was a little child from the steerage thrown overboard. I heard that it died in the night. I heard one of the passengers say that they did not box the child up or even sew it up in canvas but I should not think that they would throw it overboard without something around it. This afternoon and evening the weather was lovely. Not one bit as it was yesterday afternoon and last night.

At Sea, Thursday August 25th, 1870

This morning about half past three, we were all awakened by the ringing of the firemen's bell, the shouting of the sailors, the stoppage of the steamer, and the cry of someone apparently in distress. We were off the banks of Newfoundland and all the fuss and confusion was occasioned by our steamer running against and cutting in two, a small boat belonging to a fishing smack, called the *Lagasto Nevada* from Havre [Canada]. There were seven men in the boat but they had all fallen asleep and their light had gone out, consequently our captain did not see them and they did not see us.

As soon as possible the captain had a boat lowered and manned and they set off in search of the drowning men. They found them clinging to parts of the wrecked boat, nearly exhausted but were all picked up and brought on board. The captain gave them each a glass of grog,[3] and one of them when he drank it, smacked his lips and grinned as if he had never had any thing so good before. Then the captain asked them through an interpreter, for

3. Grog is a mixture of rum and water

they were French Canadians, which boat he should take them to, for we could see several a little way off, but they could not or would not tell, and answered "go to New York – me go to New York" so the captain gave them something to eat and a cup of coffee then gave them dry garments and sent them to bed. All this required about two hours and during the time, there was great fright and confusion among the lady passengers, worse then there was Tuesday night for when the engines stopped working and woke us all up, we thought may be the steamer was going down, down to the bottom of the fathomless sea and we were all very glad to find it otherwise.

This morning there was scarcely any wind and the water was very calm and still. Since yesterday noon we have sailed two hundred and seventy three miles. We have on board nine bishops and priests, three or four ministers and several doctors. I have not room to speak of the other passengers for there are so many and I should not know where to begin first. In the evening we had very strong rough winds again so I retired quite early.

At Sea, Friday August 26th, 1870

We have strong head winds today so do not get on so well. Since yesterday noon we have sailed two hundred and eighty miles. I remained up on deck nearly all day and amused myself watching the steamer mounting the great waves so gracefully. I do not think the vegetables are as good as they were on the *City of Antwerp* but then the vegetables etc. were bought in America and now, they were bought in England, so I suppose that is the reason we had better on board the *City of Antwerp*. This evening also, we have cold rough winds and the steamer rocks exceedingly.

At Sea, Saturday August 27th, 1870

Today also we have very rough winds. All the morning I amused myself by watching the steerage passengers. Each person is allowed only a certain quantity of water daily and this morning just as a girl had plastered her neck and face with soap preparatory for washing, the steamer gave a sudden roll and over goes the basin of water so the poor girl was obliged to wipe off the soap with her handkerchief as well as she could and postpone the use of water until the next day when she was more careful. First the girl felt and acted rather cross but when she saw that several were laughing at her, she gave in, and had a good laugh too.

About five o'clock in the afternoon the pilot came on board. Several pilots cruise around together and when they see a steamer or vessel, one of them goes to her and takes her in to New York. Our pilot was number thirteen. He said he had been out fourteen days. One of the priests is a real jolly companion. He is a very large built man and is awful savage looking but he keeps us all alive with his jokes and cute sayings. Someone asked him if he knew anything about America. He said he ought to know something about it for he lives just in the next parish with only a little Atlantic between them. This evening I had a pleasure of witnessing a clear sunset. It was really grand. The sun was just like a ball of fire, slowly sinking lower and lower and then suddenly disappearing altogether out of sight, just as if it had fallen into the ocean.

We had a lovely moonlight night and Annie Eastcott[4] and myself had a delightful walk on deck. We could see the lights of several ships off in the distance and it seemed so good to see them for they looked like a light in some window. Between yesterday noon and today noon we sailed three hundred and sixteen miles. In the evening there was scarcely any wind and the water was as calm and still as possible so the steamer glided along without rocking at all and left no track behind it.

At Sea, Sunday August 28th, 1870

To day I feel first rate and think I never felt better in health in my life. This morning after the church services were read down in the saloon, one of the ministers preached a very good sermon from the words found in first Timothy (1st chapter, 15th verse). That is the first verse I ever learned from the Bible. The singing was splendid, they all joined in with such a will. In the afternoon another gentleman preached to the steerage passengers and their singing was quite a failure. They nearly broke down two or three times. Today we have seen three or four steamers, one belonging to the Inman Line sailing for Liverpool and we have seen as many as thirty sailing vessels, some sailing for New York and others to Liverpool. About four o'clock this afternoon we could see land for an hour or so. I do not know what part of America it was, but I heard it was Long Island. We have seen several whales, but not very near.

After tea, which was very poor, for we only had tack and butter, I went up on deck and heard them singing. Some of the cabin passengers had formed a circle and were singing and it sounded splendid, but what pleased me most was last night a woman in steerage was singing a piece and it was real amusing, her voice was cracked and very coarse and she sang a long piece and oh how the steerage passengers cheered, for I suppose they thought she sang very nice and I expect she thought herself to be quite a heroine, but I am sure I could not see it in that way.

Oh dear, I shall be so glad when we get home for I am sure if I stayed aboard this ship much longer I should get so thin I should scarcely know myself for here breakfast everything is half cooked or it is scorched and I cannot eat it either way and you know I do not like coffee and the tea is boiled to death. For dinner the chicken is very tough and the other meat half cooked, but the potato and cabbage is the only thing that tastes good for the pastry is all baked and cooked too much except the rice pudding and we have only had that twice and the tea is worse still. It is miserable for the bread is sour and the butter is musty and the hard tack is hard sure enough. One can scarcely break it so all I have is hard tack, butter and cold water for the milk does not taste good so I have not had hot water but once. Now this is a good description of our meals, you see it is not anything like it was on the *City of Antwerp* and if you ask for any fruit it is ten to one if you get it. At least I find it so in my case. In the evening we could see several lighthouses and the revolving lights looked very pretty and we saw the lights of a great many ships it seemed like a town only that the lights were a good ways apart. About eight o'clock we got in sight of land again and about nine we got in the river and it was a very pretty sight to see the lights on the shore as well as a joyful sight and then the officers threw up several rockets and they went off splendid, it seemed almost like celebrating the Fourth of July.

About nine o'clock the sailors dropped anchor in New York harbor. It was a lovely evening. The moon shone very brightly and the water in the bay was very calm and peaceful. I remained up until after eleven o'clock, walking the decks in the moonlight and watching the lights on shore and I can assure you that I enjoyed myself very much indeed. After I retired I could not sleep for a long time for I felt so glad that I had once more crossed the broad Atlantic in safety and would soon be home in Rockford again. Then it seemed so queer to have the steamer at a stand still and not be rolling and pitching so. Since yesterday noon we have sailed four hundred and thirty three miles. The whole number of miles that we have sailed in crossing the deep blue Atlantic this time is three thousand and seventy four miles and we have been about ten days and a half.

The Journey Home

New York, Monday August 29th, 1870

This morning we were up bright and early reckoning to leave the *City of Paris* of the ocean not of France, but there was no hurry for we did not leave till about ten when the tender came after the cabin passengers. So we bid adieu to the good old boat that brought us across the Atlantic in safety and went aboard the tender which soon landed us safely on dry land on the company docks where the custom house officers searched all the trunks, but we got along first rate, better then I expected. They did not search very much for each gentleman had a printed declaration declaring that they had no goods for sale. Pa could not find Annie's box anywhere so we went to a hotel and Pa went back on the tender to the ship again and hunted around for over an hour and at last found it among the steerage and had it brought to the docks.

New York, Tuesday August 30th, 1870

This morning about nine o'clock the cab came for us and took us down to the ferry boat which took us over to Jersey City. We got on board a train of the Erie Railroad and were soon homeward bound. We passed through Bergen tunnel, cut through Bergen Heights. This tunnel is nearly seven-eights of a mile in length, and is encased through out with a solid arch of brickwork. About a mile beyond the tunnel there is a large oil refinery. The scenery along this route is eminently grand and imposing. For about two hundred miles the country was very hilly and reminded me very much of some parts of England. In the afternoon we stopped at one station where there were a good many soldiers all dressed in their uniforms. The Governor of New York was on the train and the soldiers fired off the cannon in honor of him. Pa bought me a book describing every place between Jersey City and Buffalo and it was real interesting to read the history of the places as we passed through them.

Traveling between New York and Home, Wednesday August 31st, 1870

Last night the baggage car got on fire so we were detained several hours and did not arrive in Cleveland until half past nine o'clock this morning and remained until about two o'clock in the afternoon. It was very warm and tiresome waiting there and we were all very glad when the train came snorting up to the station. We arrived in Toledo about eight o'clock but did not stop here very long.

Traveling, Thursday September 1st, 1870

Traveling between New York and Rockford. This morning about six o'clock we arrived in the City of Chicago. Pa went directly to the telegraph office and sent a dispatch home when we expect to reach there. About nine we left Chicago.

The journey between Chicago and Rockford seemed a very long one to me and after we had left the last station before Rockford the train seemed to go so slow, I almost wanted to get out and walk the rest of the way. At the Kishwaukee Railroad Bridge I saw Henry Baume and Frankie [Kyle], Thomas and Fannie [Lawler], William and Annie [Johns] were over to the depot to welcome us home once more. Words cannot begin to express how glad I was to see dear old Rockford and beloved friends again. The grass and trees were so fresh and green and the flowers looked so beautiful. It took us nearly three hours to eat dinner for we had so much to talk about. We brought home two baskets of delicious peaches from Chicago.

In the evening Sarah and Jennie Lake called to welcome us home, and Eva Chaney [Lucy's friends] called also. Mr. and Mrs. Congdon [Emma Giles and Thomas Congdon whose parents and family they visited in Polperro, England] and baby were up all the evening and we spent a very pleasant time telling them about their friends in Polperro, England. Frankie Congdon has grown a good deal and is real cute. He reminds me of his cousin, little Frankie Hicks.

Visit to Sister Lizzie

Wednesday September 7th, 1870

This morning we (Pa, Ma, and I) are again bidding adieu to home and friends and going off on the ten o'clock train, but we do not go with as sorrowful a heart as we did a little over four months ago. Well, we are going home with sister Lizzie to Evanston to spend a few days. We were fortunate enough to get seats together so that made it very pleasant of course. We arrived in Chicago about three o'clock p.m. and at the depot we met Mr. Baume and Annie (Baume). She has grown very much and is I think rather tall for her age.

We remained in the waiting room in the depot about an hour and were off again and very quickly the train rattled on past one station and then another till it stopped in Evanston at which place we got off and the cab took us to the present home of my sister Mrs. Elizabeth R. Baume, where we expect to remain for a few days. The boys are both very well and say they want to come to Rockford again. While we were in England, they were there a month and they enjoyed it so much they want to go again. We all spent a very pleasant evening talking about Halifax and England in general.

Thursday September 8th, 1870

This morning it was very hot, it seemed as if we could scarcely breath and so we all went down by the lake so we got cooled off a little, for you know it is always cool by the lake or ocean. About half past two a nice livery carriage and a span of pretty black horses drove up to the door and Mr. Baume, Lizzie, Pa, Ma and I went out for a nice ride and had a splendid time. We passed Calvary cemetery and Rose Hill cemetery and passed along down the road to Lincoln Park.[1] It is a beautiful place with nice drives and walks through it in every direction and little pleasure houses and grottoes and so many pretty little nooks and corners. One side was occupied by beasts. There were two large black bears and a large buffalo, three or four large deer, a wild cat, two or three white rats, an elk, several peacocks etc. And in the pretty little streams that went winding around, helping to make the place more beautiful, we saw a number of large white swans sailing about so gracefully and ducks etc. Then a part of the park went right out on the lake beach and oh, it was all truly beautiful. It really charms one. The park at Halifax was nice, what there was of it, but it does not begin to compare with Lincoln Park in size and I think it falls far below it in grandeur.

Well, we rode around here for a long time then we went around to that big city of Chicago. We passed through a good many of the principal streets, rode around the burned building of Farwell and passed through the Washington Street tunnel, a thing I have often wished to do and it seemed rather scary at first, but I soon got used to it. On our way home it rained quite hard, but we did not get wet any for we had a covered carriage. When we got nearer Evanston, we could see it had rained very much harder than where we were and in fact in the streets of Evanston the water just lay in pools. Just as we got in the house, it commenced to rain very hard again and we were glad we were safely under the shelter again. I was nearly tired out for we did not get home till

1. Lincoln Park was created in 1865 and named in honour of recently assassinated President Abraham Lincoln.

after eight o'clock.

Friday September 9th, 1870

All day today it has been awful dreary and gloomy and rainy and I felt so sleepy and stupid and half sick. I hardly knew what to do and was laying around on the sofas and chairs all day and Mr. Baume is sick too. To tell the truth I guess all of us are more then half sick. We did not go out of the house all day, but I suppose we were gone enough yesterday for today too. I did not remain up very late for I did not sleep any too well last night so I retired to rest after Annie (Baume) did and I room with her.

Saturday, September 10th, 1870

This morning by the forty-five minute past train Pa, Ma, and I started for home again and sister Lizzie went in to Chicago with us. We had a nice eleven mile ride and got in Chicago about ten o'clock and we walked right over to Mrs. Leonard's and found them well as usual. Mr. Leonard is in Canada spending a few weeks. We remained there to dinner and then went down town. We went through a good many of the principal streets and saw some very handsome buildings as good or better then any I saw in England. Hamlin's store is a splendid one, a great deal better then any in England for I did not see one store or shop as they call them that had separate counters for separate things, such as a counter for lace, a certain counter for silks, another for velvets, another for ribbons, another for fancy things, another for dry goods and so on etc. and there were counters for every thing you could think of in the dress and dressing line. Now I saw nothing of the sort while we were in England.

Everybody says that all our best and fancy goods come from England, but we found out it was no such thing for we could not find any thing in that line as nice and pretty as we can get in America, the place where nearly all of the English people think that we cannot even get the base necessities of life much more any thing else. That America is inhabited principally by a low barbarian set who would as soon kill and eat each other as anything else and that is was not safe for a stranger to come here at all. I guess if they came here they would find every thing entirely different from what they had supposed. They also said our Republican Government would not and could not stand (the very idea is perfectly absurd). They acknowledged that if it did stand it would be the strongest in the world and would rule all other nations, but they did not want that so they said they knew it would break down not many years hence. They said it was not destined to stand in the first place and therefore it would not. But never mind, we shall see one of these days which government will stand, for American or the English and we know now that the Republican Government of the United States will stand as long as time is.

Well, I have wandered from my subject. After we had done a little shopping we went to the depot and waited till four o'clock then bid good-bye to sister Lizzie. We were soon off again. Lizzie started a quarter past four for Evanston. We got home at half past eight and Tom, Fan and Frankie met us with the carriage. We found them all well.

* * * * *

And now we are home again from our wanderings on a foreign shore, I will close my beloved journal that I have taken so much pleasure in writing. I will say Farewell, hoping to enjoy a good many hours in perusing its contents.

Lucy C. Rodd, Rockford, Illinois

Epilogue

Less than three years after her visit to England, Lucy Rodd died of tuberculosis in the 'brick house' in Rockford in March, 1873, shortly before her 18th birthday. No official death records were kept at the time and only a brief newspaper announcement of her death survives.

Lucy and her parents were founding members of the Centennial Methodist Church in Rockford and a large stained glass window was installed there by her parents in her memory. She lies buried on a hill in Rockford's Cedar Bluff Cemetery with other members of her family (her father died in 1884 and her mother in 1896 at the age of 89).

One of Lucy's sisters, Ann Rodd, married William Johns (referred to by Lucy as Brother William). Their eleven children became the line that is the extended Johns family in Illinois and the extended Brown family in Canada. In 1907, Lucy's niece Fannie Brown took the original diary with her to Canada. Today it remains the treasured possession of the Rodd family descendants who hope you have enjoyed traveling with Lucy as she met with family and friends on her epic journey.

Appendix

Rodd family relations referred to in Lucy's Diary

Baume, Elizabeth (neé Rodd), Lucy's sister, married to Rev. James Baume; Evanston, Illinois, USA
Baume, Henry, Lucy's nephew and son of James and stepson of Elizabeth (neé Rodd) Baume; Evanston, Illinois, USA
Baume, James, Lucy's brother-in-law, married to sister Elizabeth (Lizzie); Evanston, Illinois, USA
Baume, John, relative of Lucy's brother-in-law James Baume; Halifax, Yorkshire, England
Clement, Catherine, sister of Christopher Clement; Alwington, Devon, England
Clement, Christopher, son of Lucy's mother's cousin, Joseph Clement; Bideford, Devon, England
Clement, Elizabeth, daughter of Lucy's mother's cousin, Joseph Clement; Halwell, Devon, England
Clement, Jane (neé Squance), Lucy's grandmother; Parkham, Devon, England
Clement, John, Lucy's mother's cousin and brother of Christopher Clement; Canada
Clement, Joseph, Lucy's mother's cousin; Halwell, Devon, England
Elwick, Mary (neé Johns), sister of Elizabeth, Richard, Thomas and William Johns, married to John Elwick; Rockford, Illinois, USA
Fiddick, Elizabeth (neé Johns), sister of Mary, Richard, Thomas, and William Johns, married to James Fiddick; Cornwall, England
Gerry, Mary (neé Rodd), Lucy's aunt and sister to Joseph Rodd, married to Richard Gerry; Pyworthy, Devon, England
Gerry, Richard, Lucy's uncle; Pyworthy, Devon, England
Johns, Ann (neé Rodd), Lucy's sister, married to William Johns, Rockford, Illinois, USA
Johns, Ella, Lucy's niece and daughter of William and Ann (neé Rodd) Johns; Rockford Illinois, USA
Johns, Elizabeth (neé Ede), wife of Thomas Johns; Polperro, Cornwall, England
Johns, Emma, daughter of Richard and Jane (neé Hocken) Johns; Rockford, Illinois, USA
Johns, Fannie Mary, Lucy's niece and daughter of William and Ann (neé Rodd) Johns; Rockford Illinois, USA

Johns, Freddie, Lucy's nephew and son of sister Ann (neé Rodd) and William Johns; Rockford, Illinois, USA
Johns, Georgie, Lucy's nephew and son of sister Ann (neé Rodd) and William Johns; Rockford, Illinois, USA
Johns, Jane (neé Hocken), wife of Richard Johns; Rockford Illinois, USA
Johns, Mary, daughter of Thomas and Elizabeth (neé Ede) Johns; Polperro, Cornwall, England
Johns, Thomas, Lucy's cousin and brother of William Johns; Polperro, Cornwall, England
Johns, William, Lucy's brother-in-law, married to sister Ann (neé Rodd); Rockford, Illinois, USA
Kyle, Frankie, Lucy's nephew and son of sister Mary Jane (neé Rodd) Kyle; Rockford, Illinois, USA
Lawler, Fannie (neé Rodd), Lucy's sister, married to Thomas Lawler; Rockford, Illinois, USA
Lawler, Thomas, Lucy's brother-in-law, married to sister Fannie (neé Rodd); Rockford, Illinois, USA
Main, Eva, daughter of Martha Main; Northam, Devon, England
Main, Martha (neé Withecombe), Lucy's cousin and daughter of Fannie and William Withecombe; Northam, Devon, England
Rodd, Fannie, Lucy's cousin and daughter of John Rodd; Instow, Devon, England
Rodd, John, Lucy's uncle and brother to Joseph Rodd; Instow, Devon, England
Rodd, Joseph, (Pa) father of Lucy; Rockford, Illinois, USA
Rodd, Lucy Clement; Rockford, Illinois, USA
Rodd, Mary (neé Gerry), married to Lucy's uncle Richard Rodd and sister of Richard Gerry; Launceston, Cornwall, England
Rodd, Mary (neé Creeper), Lucy's grandmother and wife of Thomas Rodd; Pyworthy, Devon, England
Rodd, Mary Ann (neé Clement), (Ma) mother of Lucy; Rockford, Illinois, USA
Rodd, Mary Ann, Lucy's cousin and daughter of John Rodd; Instow, Devon, England
Rodd, Sarah, Lucy's aunt and second wife of John Rodd; Instow, Devon, England
Rodd, Thomas, Lucy's cousin and son of John Rodd; Instow, Devon, England
Rodd, Thomas, Lucy's grandfather and husband of Mary (neé Creeper) Rodd; Pyworthy, Devon, England
Rodd, William, Lucy's uncle and brother of Joseph Rodd; Pyworthy, Devon, England

Withecombe, Ann (neé Hookway), Lucy's cousin, married to Robert Withecombe; Buckland Brewer, Devon, England

Withecombe, Charles, Lucy's cousin and son of aunt Fannie (neé Clement) and William Withecombe; Buckland Brewer, Devon, England

Withecombe, Ellen, Lucy's cousin and daughter of aunt Fannie (neé Clement) and William Withecombe; Buckland Brewer, Devon, England

Withecombe, Fannie (neé Clement), Lucy's aunt, married to William Withecombe; Buckland Brewer, Devon, England

Withecombe, Robert, Lucy's cousin and son of aunt Fannie (neé Clement) and William Withecombe; Buckland Brewer, Devon, England

Withecombe, William, Lucy's uncle, married to Fannie (neé Clement); Buckland Brewer, Devon, England

The Johns family of Polperro who emigrated to North America in the 19th century

Thomas **JOHNS** 1803-1879
m. Elizabeth LIGHTFOOT 1824 Polperro
Emigrated to Rockford, Illinois 1851 | 1803-1885

- Jane 1824-1916 *m.* George HAYCRAFT
  Emigrated to Canada 1851
- Elizabeth 1826-1914 *m.* James FIDDICK
  Emigrated to Rockford, Illinois 1874
- Richard 1828-1911 *m.* Jane Ann HOCKEN
  Emigrated to Rockford, Illinois 1850
- Thomas 1830-1904 *m.* Elizabeth EDE
  Remained in Polperro
- William 1832-1926 *m.* Ann RODD*
  Emigrated to Rockford, Illinois 1851
- Priscilla 1836-1927 *m.* Charles HALEY
  Emigrated to Rockford, Illinois 1851
- Mary 1839-1903 *m.* John ELWICK
  Emigrated to Rockford, Illinois 1851
- Ann 1842-1902 *m.* Thomas JOHNS
  Emigrated to Rockford, Illinois 1851

*Sister to Lucy Rodd